A CASSELL CARAVEL BOOK

PHARAOHS
OF EGYPT

By the Editors of
HORIZON MAGAZINE

Author
JACQUETTA HAWKES

Consultant
BERNARD V. BOTHMER

Curator, Department of Ancient Art, The Brooklyn Museum

ILLUSTRATED WITH RELIEFS, SCULPTURES,
WALL PAINTINGS, AND MONUMENTS OF ANCIENT EGYPT

Cassell · London

© 1965 by American Heritage Publishing Co,, Inc., 551 Fifth Avenue, New York 17,
New York. All rights reserved under Berne and Pan-American Copyright Conventions.
Trademark CARAVEL registered United States Patent Office
First published in Great Britain 1967. Second impression 1970.
Printed and bound in Italy by Arnoldo Mondadori Editore
I.S.B.N. 0 304 92583 7

FOREWORD

The history of ancient Egypt is written not in colourful narratives but in colossal statues, in vast temples whose walls are covered with hieroglyphic inscriptions, and in tomb objects whose value and brilliance remain undiminished after five thousand years.

Such staggeringly huge and rich monuments have been both a curse and a blessing. The monuments, for all their impressiveness, seem at first glance like bombastic advertisements; they have persuaded generations of viewers that the Pharaohs who ruled Egypt from 2686 to 1085 B.C. were too grand to be believed, too removed in place and time to possess any meaning for our Western culture. It was only in this century, when the painstaking work of linguists, art scholars, and archaeologists combined to give a detailed and non-monumental picture of ancient Egypt, that the Pharaohs' unique role in world history could be fully appreciated.

The Pharaohs' greatest achievements occurred during the period known as the New Kingdom (1567 to 1085 B.C.), and that period therefore receives the closest attention in this book. Jacquetta Hawkes' narrative takes advantage of the most recent scholarship: it looks at the behind-the-scenes life of the Pharaohs as well as their ceremonial existence and their military conquests, and it concludes with a chapter on the exciting new science that Egyptology has become. The wall paintings, reliefs, and statues that are also included in these pages further illustrate the highly personal, even eccentric, quality of the Pharaohs' reigns.

It is the Pharaohs' peculiar sovereignty that emerges as the most impressive theme of ancient Egypt—by their individual genius they guided the world's first great civilization. That human story, now that it can be told with greater realism and accuracy, may outlast any of the towering structures that were once erected against the wind and sands of time.

THE EDITORS

Pictures and hieroglyphs celebrating the reign of one of Egypt's greatest rulers were originally contained within this beautifully painted mural frame. It is thought that a jealous successor had the signs hacked from the wall.

HIRMER VERLAG, MUNICH

7

In this tomb mural, an official pours a libation of wine over meal and game. Egyptian painters believed that the human form, with the exception of the torso, was best shown from the side. Accordingly, the head, arms, hands, legs, and feet of the figures are in profile. The chest is shown frontally.

COVER: *The solid gold funeral mask of King Tutankhamon gives a suggestion of the splendour and riches of the powerful New Kingdom Pharaohs.*

ENDPAPERS: *In two scenes from a painted chest in Tutankhamon's tomb the young king is charging Egypt's ancient foes the Nubians and Syrians.*

TITLE PAGE: *This amulet, whose design appears throughout Egyptian art, represents the god Horus' eye. It ensured protection and fertility.*

BACK COVER: *Egypt's wealth came from farming and trade, but tribute and taxes supported the Pharaohs. Here Syrians are shown with gifts.*

CONTENTS

	FOREWORD	7
I	PEOPLE OF THE NILE	10
II	KINGS AND GODS	34
III	BUILDERS OF EMPIRE	52
IV	SPLENDOUR AND REVOLUTION	72
V	CONQUERORS' DECLINE	96
VI	GOLD OF THE PHARAOHS	120
	ACKNOWLEDGMENTS	148
	FURTHER REFERENCE	149
	INDEX	150

I

PEOPLE OF
THE NILE

The Pharaohs of Egypt led their country out of the Stone Age to heights of cultural achievement that have rarely, if ever, been matched in human history. There were, in effect, three peaks of ancient Egyptian culture—called the Old Kingdom (2686 to 2181 B.C.), the Middle Kingdom (2133 to 1786 B.C.), and the New Kingdom (1567 to 1085 B.C.)—each one of which was characterized by a grandeur and a passion all its own.

Remarkable and impressive as were the royal leaders who produced these extraordinary periods, neither they nor Egyptian culture can be understood without an appreciation of the supreme importance of the River Nile. Winding like a serpent throughout the length of the land, the river has always provided an abundance of food for Egyptians: it did so in the prehistoric past, in the time of the Pharaohs, and does up to the present day. The Nile supplied the Pharaohs and their subjects with a way of travelling and communicating; it greatly affected their political systems and religious beliefs. The kingdom could never had been held together without this tremendous waterway (see map on page 16).

The river rises in the lake country of central Africa, where the White Nile begins its long journey northward to the Mediterranean Sea. At Khartoum the White Nile is joined by the turbulent waters of the Blue Nile, racing down from the Ethiopian highlands. Two hundred miles farther north, the mountain-born Atbara pours its floodwaters into the main stream, and from that point, the Nile

The great pyramids of Giza, on the outskirts of Cairo, proclaim the timeless grandeur of three ancient Pharaohs: Cheops (background), Chephren (centre), and Mycerinus (in front, with smaller pyramids for his family).

Lively scenes of men at work and at war in ancient Egypt have been found on the walls of temples and tombs. Many of these scenes are sculptures in relief—that is, not fully moulded but partially carved out of a background. One such relief is at left: fishermen haul in a catch from the Nile with a net.

flows, unsupported by any other water source, across seventeen hundred miles of desert to the sea.

Between Khartoum and Aswan, the steady course of the river is interrupted six times by veins of granite that run across the river bed, forming broken, rock-studded rapids, or cataracts. Just below Cairo, the Nile forms a huge delta, and finally, by two widely separate channels, the river enters the sea.

Although the desert through which the river flows is barren, the valley of the Nile is one of the most fertile in the world. On either side, the banks of the river are rich with thousands of years' deposit of black mud and silt, borne down from the high Ethiopian plateaux by the Blue Nile. Each year, during the early weeks of July, the Blue Nile, swollen with spring rains and melting snows, becomes a raging torrent, scouring rocks and boulders from its bed and pouring immense volumes of water into the placid body of the White Nile. Then the combined waters begin to rise over the whole length of the river, flooding its banks and depositing the silt that renews the land. It is this annual inundation—the gift of the Nile—that gives the land its miraculous fertility.

The civilization that flourished by the Nile has had an extraordinarily long history. Even when the first Pharaoh won his throne (3100 B.C.), the Egyptian people and their characteristic habits of life had been taking shape for many centuries.

By about 8000 B.C. the glaciers and ice sheets that had covered so much of northern Europe and Asia during the Ice Age were melting away as the climate grew warmer. One result of this retreat of the ice was to make the course of the moisture-laden Atlantic winds shift northward. Before that time there had always been a good rainfall in North Africa, and much of the Sahara and what is now desert country adjoining the Nile were well enough watered to support a teeming variety of animal life. There were elephants, giraffes, buffalo, and rhinoceroses, as well as many kinds of small game.

There were also human beings who lived by hunting the animals. At this time men were still entirely dependent on stone for their arrowheads and their other tools and weapons; and they had no knowledge of farming. That is, they were in the Paleolithic (Old Stone Age) stage of culture. As the rainfall grew less and less, grass and other vegetation dried out, and the game animals could no longer find enough food. Some must have gradually withdrawn to the south, where many species still survive, but others crowded to the few areas where water supplies remained—and of these areas the largest was the Nile valley itself.

Between 8000 and 5000 B.C., then, the Paleolithic hunters and their game animals became concentrated in the Nile valley, the small valleys running down into it, and the big lake in the Fayum Depression, which ran along its western side. These hunters were to form part of the ancestry of the historic Egyptians.

Meanwhile, in south-west Asia, men were responding to the climate changes in a more resourceful way. While still using stone for their implements, they started to cultivate cereals, to domesticate cattle and sheep, and to settle in villages—so developed the Neolithic period. After a long

The relief below shows a dispute along the river. At lower right one man is trying to gouge a hole in his opponents' boat while the others battle it out with sticks.

period of development, some of these Neolithic (New Stone Age) farmers reclaimed and irrigated the great valley of the Rivers Tigris and Euphrates. Here, in Mesopotamia, civilized life in cities first began.

Though separated from Mesopotamia by difficult desert country, the Nile valley was not very far from the fringes of the pioneer farming area of south-west Asia. It was inevitable that the Neolithic way of life would soon spread to Egypt.

It seems to have been about 5000 B.C. that farming first began to be adopted by former hunting peoples in the Nile valley; people who had learned the techniques of agriculture spread into Egypt from Palestine and Syria. For although the early Egyptian cattle may have been native, the sheep were certainly of Asiatic origin, as were the wheat and barley.

By the time Egypt's prehistoric hunters had turned to farming, the people of the Nile were no longer racially separate from the rest of the world—if they ever had been. Though in the far distant past the Egyptians may have formed a distinct part of the brown Mediterranean race, they gradually absorbed other elements. In the south it appears that intermixture with the people of the African deserts and uplands occurred more or less continuously; in the north there were increasing contacts with people from both Libya and western Asia as time went on. The language of ancient Egypt, therefore, was an astonishing collection of borrowings from all points of the compass.

Between 4000 and 3000 B.C. (the fourth millennium), the bottom of the Nile valley was still marshy and was inhabited by countless flocks of water fowl as well as crocodiles and hippopotamuses. Between the Western and Eastern Deserts, the valley was soggy, with reed-filled swamps and shallow ponds, or water holes, left by the yearly Nile flood. But in the north the delta region was well drained and extremely fertile, surrounded on each side of its fan by rich meadowland. Many of the first farming villages were built on the edges of the desert above the valley or around the Fayum Depression, which had become a large, fertile oasis in the Libyan plateau a few miles west of the Nile. During the next several centuries, the valley and the delta filled with silt, while the water level continued to drop. As the layers of silt created more and more land that could be cultivated, the farmers moved farther down into the valley lowlands and began to reclaim the soil.

Once the river had settled in its bed, farming was no

TEXT CONTINUED ON PAGE 18

PHOTO ROGER WOOD: COURTESY THAMES & HUDSON

As in centuries past, the Nile today is bounded by green strips of land made fertile by the annual flooding. Beyond are the sands of the desert.

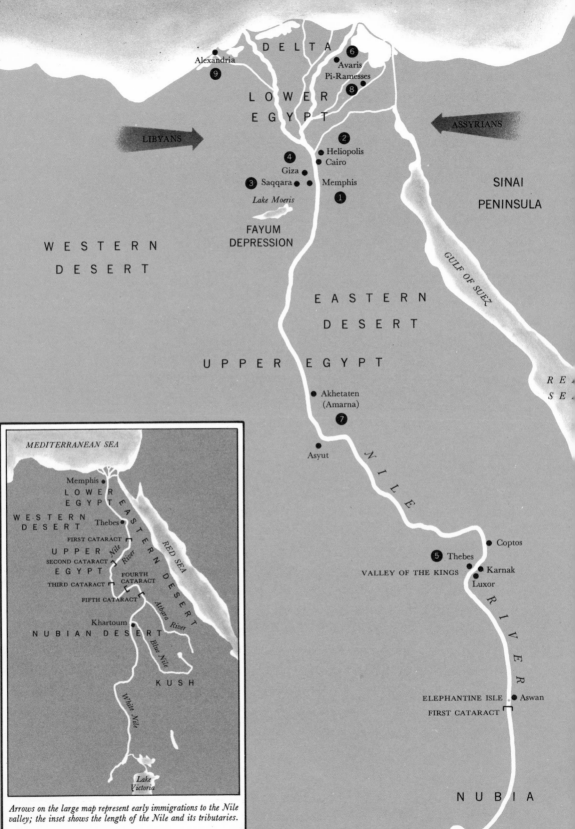

MEDITERRANEAN SEA

DELTA

Alexandria
9

LOWER

EGYPT

6
Avaris
Pi-Ramesses
8

2

Heliopolis
Cairo

4
Giza

3 Saqqara
Memphis
1

Lake Moeris

FAYUM
DEPRESSION

LIBYANS

ASSYRIANS

SINAI

PENINSULA

WESTERN

DESERT

GULF OF SUEZ

EASTERN

DESERT

UPPER EGYPT

Akhetaten
(Amarna)
7

Asyut

NILE

RE
SE

Coptos

5 Thebes

VALLEY OF THE KINGS

Karnak

Luxor

RIVER

ELEPHANTINE ISLE

Aswan

FIRST CATARACT

NUBIA

MEDITERRANEAN SEA

Memphis
LOWER
EGYPT
Thebes

WESTERN
DESERT

FIRST CATARACT

UPPER
SECOND CATARACT
EGYPT

THIRD CATARACT

EASTERN DESERT

Nile
River

RED SEA

FOURTH
CATARACT

FIFTH CATARACT

Atbara River

Khartoum

NUBIAN DESERT

Blue Nile

KUSH

White Nile

Lake
Victoria

Arrows on the large map represent early immigrations to the Nile valley; the inset shows the length of the Nile and its tributaries.

THE TWO LANDS—GIFT OF THE RIVER

The Nile—flowing through the desert of Upper Egypt and the delta of Lower Egypt—gave life to the people of the river. On the chronological chart below and on the map at left, the civilization the Egyptians established, and its essential relation to the river, has been traced back to 5000 B.C.

THE PRE-DYNASTIC PERIOD When the last glacier of the ice age receded, North Africa was left dry and turned into desert. Farming along the Nile probably started around 5000 B.C., and villages appeared along the valley in 3600 B.C. The country was first unified around 3100 B.C. by Narmer, who founded the family of rulers now

called the First Dynasty. His capital was in Memphis (marked 1 on the map). Taxes, accounting, and writing evolved, and astronomers in Heliopolis (2) invented a calendar, which enabled the Egyptian farmers to predict the season of the life-giving Nile's floods.

THE OLD KINGDOM The Third Dynasty began in 2686 B.C., but Zoser (2666–2647 B.C.) was the first characteristic Old Kingdom Pharaoh. He and his vizier, Imhotep, raised the first pyramid in Saqqara (3). In 2589 B.C., the Fourth Dynasty Pharaoh Cheops began his reign and constructed his giant pyramid at Giza (4). Chephren, who followed in 2558 B.C., built a second pyramid and erected the Sphinx. Other tombs were built after

this, but none were so great. In the Fifth Dynasty, the Egyptians won wars in Asia, but the central ruling power was greatly weakened. Provincial governors grew stronger, and after the long rule of Pepy II (died 2180 B.C.), there followed a time of chaos and social upheaval now called the First Intermediate Period. Famine ravaged the land, and men's minds turned to justice and virtue.

THE MIDDLE KINGDOM The Theban prince Mentuhotep II, founder of the Eleventh Dynasty, organized Upper Egypt and conquered the rich delta country, called Lower Egypt. He moved the royal court to Thebes (5). These events in 2040 B.C. marked the beginning of the Middle Kingdom. Trade flourished over the sea to Crete and

across the desert of Sinai; painting, crafts, and sculpture developed energetically. A time of Asian rule, called the Second Intermediate Period, under the Hyksos kings in Avaris (6), came to a violent end in 1567 B.C. The court returned to Thebes, and the two kingdoms were reunited.

THE NEW KINGDOM In 1525 B.C., Tuthmosis I began his militaristic reign, leading his armies to the banks of the Euphrates. He was succeeded by his son, Tuthmosis II, and his daughter, Hatshepsut. Tuthmosis II ruled only briefly, but Hatshepsut shared the throne with her stepson, Tuthmosis III. It was a peaceful period of building and trade until she died in 1482 B.C. When Tuthmosis III assumed full power, he re-established his grandfather's frontiers and spent half his time in the field with his armies. In 1417 B.C., Amenhotep III ascended the throne, and word of Egypt's great wealth spread throughout the world. He was succeeded by the brilliant Akhenaten in 1379 B.C., and the worship of the Aten as the only true god was initiated. Art and kingship became more personal, and life in the new capital, Akhetaten (7),

was progressive and humane. In the Nineteenth Dynasty, the capital was moved to Pi-Ramesses (8). This period (1320–1200 B.C.) was dominated by Seti I and Ramesses II, the tireless builder. Ramesses III was the last great Pharaoh, but the eight Ramesses who followed him were less fortunate, and less distinguished. Ramesses XI died in 1085 B.C., and the New Kingdom came to an end.

A long period of division followed, and it was not until 332 B.C. that a strong central government took hold. Even then, it was imposed by a foreigner, Alexander the Great, who installed the Macedonian Ptolemies in his city, Alexandria (9). They reigned until Queen Cleopatra died in 30 B.C., and Egypt fell into the hands of the Roman Caesar Augustus.

TEXT CONTINUED FROM PAGE 14

longer so precarious, for the Nile flood was as regular as a clock, and highly beneficial to the land. The energetic pioneers learned to drain the swamps and to devise ways of irrigating their fields. At first, all their time and efforts were spent in making the land arable, in growing and harvesting the crops, and in looking after their livestock. As farming methods improved and the food supply became abundant, the population began to expand, and men began to have time for other activities. By 3600 B.C. village settlements had grown into sizable towns, and within the next five hundred years, into true cities with many fine public buildings.

The predictable and unchanging patterns in the behaviour of the Nile may have helped the ancient Egyptians to believe in a strictly formed social order. The order of their political and spiritual life imitated the rhythmic regularity of the most important forces in their natural world, and they wanted the life and death of men to have

18

Stone Age farmers along the Nile founded a vigorous civilization, which can be glimpsed through its artifacts. The female figure with arms upraised on the opposite page is a dancing goddess made in that pre-dynastic period; the disc with the dogs and gazelles was part of a game. The contemporary objects shown above are more practical but no less decorative: a comb topped by a hippopotamus, a flint knife with a relief of battling warriors, and a pot graced by a river boat.

the same harmony as the regular cycle of the seasons.

A strong desire for order does not, however, rule out change, and there was experimentation and progress, both social and technical, in those early days.

Although Egypt had from its beginning been divided into two parts, it was held together throughout most of its history by the force of strong rulers—and by the Nile itself. Upper Egypt refers to the long river valley from the First Cataract near Aswan down along the length of the Nile to the ancient city of Memphis; Lower Egypt extends from Memphis through the delta region to the coast of the Mediterranean Sea.

In both Upper and Lower Egypt, small, separate communities were grouped into clan areas. Such areas, or districts, were made up of groups of villages surrounding a capital town. They were led by a powerful chieftain and were protected by their own particular god, each with his own distinctive emblems. At an early period, the districts of the south and those of the north banded together into two separate kingdoms, each under the leadership of the prince of its most powerful unit. These clan areas are an interesting example of the continuity of Egyptian society, for they survived, to emerge in historic times as the administrative units known as nomes. In the nome, the clan chief had become a governor appointed by the Pharaoh—the god-king—usually from among the local dignitaries. The governor resided in a capital town that also contained the chief temple of the local deity. In this way several of the prehistoric divinities and their emblems found their way into the Egyptian pantheon. By the time of the New Kingdom era in the middle of the second millennium B.C., there were forty-two nomes in Upper and Lower Egypt.

New developments and techniques also began to appear in the artistic expressions of these prehistoric Egyptians. Gifted craftsmen, they began now to use gold and copper and to carve elegant ivory combs and knife handles, to shape stone vases, and to make slate palettes in the forms of fish, turtles, and birds, which they used first for grinding eye paint and later as memorial or ceremonial plaques. Already, among these peasant societies of the fourth millennium B.C., who were still living in what was essentially a Stone Age economy, the cultural "style" of the future glories of Egyptian civilization was beginning to emerge.

During this period of their development, the people of the Nile received a further cultural stimulus from Asia.

TEXT CONTINUED ON PAGE 22

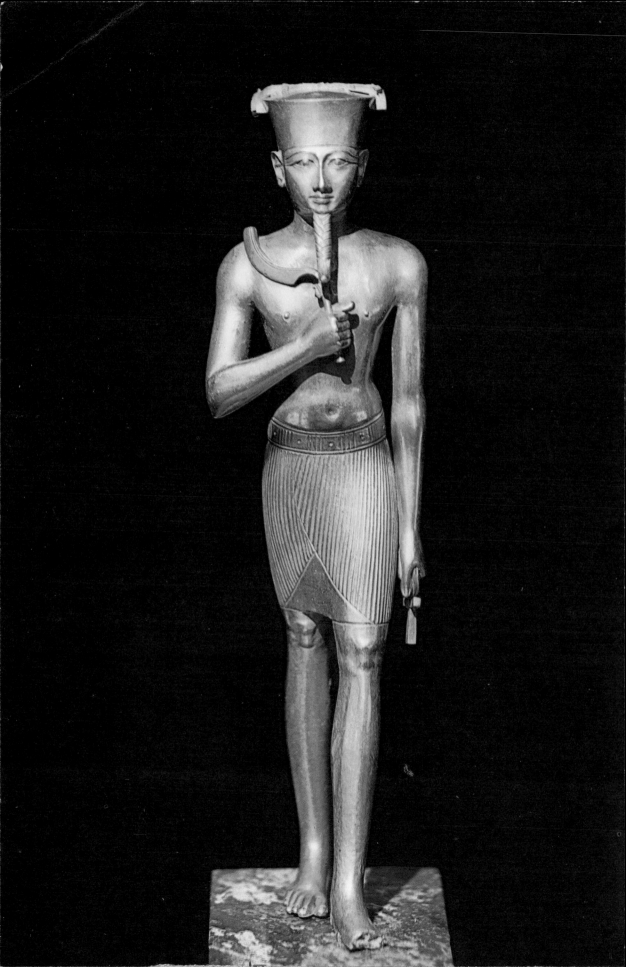

GODS OF THE SUN

When Herodotus described the Egyptians as "religious to excess, beyond any other nation in the world", he spoke of the practices of his own era, the fifth century B.C. The staggering fervour of the dynastic times had passed away, and what remained for Herodotus to comment upon amounted to little more than a shadowy imitation of the great days of Egyptian divine worship. Of all the gods and goddesses worshipped on the Nile, the most important were the gods of the sun. Sometimes their names were different, and their personalities altered with the times, but their identification with the sun remained constant. The first and most enduring of these gods was Re, depicted with a falcon's head and a bull's tail on the wood stela shown above. Re appeared in the Second Dynasty and enjoyed his first real popularity during the construction of the pyramids at Giza, where each tomb

was capped with gold to reflect his rays as he passed overhead. The falcon was a symbol of the god Horus, with whom Re was often combined and called Re-Horakhty: On the right, a woman makes her offering of food and papyrus as rays of sunlight in the form of flowers bless her. The golden statuette opposite represents Amon, the sun god of the Theban warriors who drove the Hyksos kings from Egypt. He holds a scimitar in his right hand, the Key of Life in his left; the double feather of his crown is broken off. Amon's very popularity and prestige were occasionally troublesome, for his priests became so powerful that the Pharaohs felt threatened by them. Nevertheless, the Pharaohs did everything possible to imitate Amon, and during each new reign, artists tended to put the face of the Pharaoh on statues of Amon; the king, naturally, felt that he possessed the divine might of the god.

TEXT CONTINUED FROM PAGE 19

The Nile delta has always been one of the crossroads of the eastern Mediterranean world. Here, the Egyptians met and exchanged ideas with the island people of Cyprus, Rhodes, and Crete, with Semites from Palestine and Syria, and with the peoples of the civilizations between the Rivers Tigris and Euphrates. Regular trade with such eastern Mediterranean ports as Byblos probably began, and sailing vessels steered by rudders plied their way along the coasts of the sea, carrying goods and embassies and ideas between Egypt and the other eastern Mediterranean civilizations.

In Egypt, changes were now taking place rapidly. The power of the chieftains grew, and the more ambitious ones, particularly in Upper Egypt, began to assert themselves over their neighbours. Reclaiming and irrigation of the land became better organized, and the population must have increased rapidly. Before, most villages had been little clusters of huts made of matting or reeds, but now sun-dried mud brick was adopted and was used both for houses and for handsome temples and chieftains' dwellings. At this time, the use of writing began to develop; possibly it was introduced from Asia, although the Egyptians, from the beginning, devised their own picture signs.

Then, in about the year 3100 B.C., a great political advance was made. Narmer, one of the conquering chieftains of Upper Egypt, who must have been a man of extraordinary ability both as a soldier and a statesman, succeeded in uniting all the nomes of both Upper and Lower Egypt into a single kingdom. Thus, the kingdom of Egypt was created, united physically by its great navigable river and spiritually by its first divine Pharaoh.

Narmer is known to us from a finely carved palette showing his conquests and inscribed with one of the earliest Egyptian picture writings. It seems that he must have been the same person as Menes, who, in the semi-legendary chronicles of early Egypt, is credited with unifying Egypt and founding its first royal dynasty.

Not very much is known of the first two dynasties, which together make up the early dynastic period. In order to foster political unity, Narmer built his capital at Memphis, near the meeting point of Upper and Lower Egypt, and the Pharaohs who succeeded him lived there also. In order to keep track of their property and to administer the business of the government, the formal picture signs, called hieroglyphs, were abbreviated into a form of handwriting, and a kind of paper was invented; it was

King Narmer, unifier of Egypt and founder of the First Dynasty, is portrayed in relief on a commemorative palette. Wearing the crown of Lower Egypt, the king prepares to strike the enemy at his feet. The small figure on the left side of the palette is a servant who is holding Narmer's sacred sandals.

made from the flattened and dried pith of the papyrus reed. Astronomy, valuable for calculating the date of the flood, was developed, especially at the centre of sun worship, Heliopolis, about twenty miles north of Memphis. And to pay for the administration of a unified land, a system of levying taxes in grain and other produce was established. It was to remain for thousands of years a burdensome part of the Egyptian peasant's life.

The first two royal dynasties are believed to have covered fourteen reigns lasting approximately 415 years. It was a time of preparation not only in the strengthening of government and in the intellectual life of the elite, but in developing technical skills. Copper working was mastered, and the metal was used for handsome vessels and implements; so too was the cutting of hard stones. A glazed composition pottery, today called faience, was invented and was to enliven Egyptian craftsmanship for thousands of years. In fact, the "style" of the civilization was now established. There would be many additions to the range of Egyptian culture, but from this time on it would have its own distinct character.

The Third Dynasty, which ruled Egypt during the first half of the third millennium B.C., marked the beginning of that period in Egyptian history known as the Old Kingdom. In this period came the sudden flowering of culture for which the advances of the early dynastic times had prepared the way. In the middle of this third dynastic

The Step Pyramid at Saqqara was the first of the great royal pyramids. Built by the master architect Imhotep for King Zoser, it was surrounded by a huge complex of ceremonial buildings, including the ruined temple in the foreground.

In this relief from the wall of Zoser's Step Pyramid, the king is shown running a ceremonial race with the ritual flail in his hand.

period there lived an extraordinary genius named Imhotep. He was the vizier, or chief official, of the Pharaoh Zoser, who came to the throne in 2666 B.C. Imhotep's enormous talents made such an impression on his countrymen that he was, much later, worshipped as a god. He seems to have been famous as a writer, healer, and man of universal wisdom, but his most lasting achievement was as an architect. He built a tremendous tomb for his royal master in which he not only initiated an architecture in stone, but the idea of the monumental pyramid. Zoser's Step Pyramid is at Saqqara, on the desert edge just to the west of Memphis, where many Pharaohs after him were buried. Imhotep did not build the perfect, smooth-sided pyramid of later centuries but created the general form by piling six rectangular stages one above another, each smaller than the one below. This extraordinary pile, two hundred feet high, is still standing, together with its lofty enclosure wall, its courts, and its temples. The buildings are made of small stone blocks, evidently copied from the old mud bricks that had been used for buildings in the late pre-dynastic times. Columns were made to imitate the bundles of papyrus stems that had been used in pre-dynastic reed buildings, while the capitals (the tops of the columns) were decorated with hanging umbels, or flower clusters. Some of the rooms were lined with blue faience tiles made to look like rush matting. These early dynastic buildings were stone replicas of the interlaced twig, brick, and reed architecture of the past. With their great fondness for things of the past, the Egyptian architects held to this tradition for century after century. Even in the time of the New Kingdom, more than a thousand years later, the columns and capitals of the gigantic temples were still based on the shapes of reeds and of lotus and palm trees.

The pyramid built to house Zoser's body was entirely surrounded by a mile-long wall of funerary buildings; this was the first major effort at building in stone ever attempted by man. It must have made everyone marvel— and it confirmed them in their faith that the Pharaoh, the owner of such a burial place, must indeed be a god. Even more astonishing buildings were to follow Imhotep's creation. With the Fourth Dynasty, which came to power about 2613 B.C., the Pharaohs raised three stupendous pyramids at Giza. Many centuries later, the Greeks listed the pyramids among the Seven Wonders of the World, wonders that included the Hanging Gardens of Babylon, the statue of Zeus at Olympia, the Temple of Diana at

Later Pharaohs represented themselves more grandly than Zoser ever presumed to. Above are the Sphinx and the pyramid of Chephren; the face of the Sphinx was battered by cannon fire in the Middle Ages.

Ephesus, the Mausoleum of Halicarnassus, the Colossus of Rhodes, and the lighthouse at Alexandria. Among all of these great works of man, the pyramids were the most admired, and they alone still remain standing, forty-five centuries later.

The largest of the pyramids at Giza, the tomb of Cheops, second king of the Fourth Dynasty, is still the most massive single building in existence, covering thirteen acres. By this time architects had learned how to construct a perfect pyramidal form. They no longer used small stones but shaped massive slabs of rock into building blocks. Two million such blocks weighing up to fifteen tons each went into the Great Pyramid of Cheops. The surface of the pyramid was polished, and the apex was probably capped with gold, so that from miles away peasants in the fields or nomads crossing the desert were able to see the great symbol of the sun gleaming against the sky and recognize the superhuman power of the Pharaoh lying in the darkness of his chamber at the heart of the pyramid.

Temples and tombs clustered around the pyramids were full of sculptured figures and scenes carved in relief. The head of Hemiunu, the architect of Cheops' pyramid, is a masterpiece of real-life portraiture; the seated figure of Chephren, for whom the second pyramid at Giza was built, is full of a calm nobility. The reliefs, especially those of the tombs of the Fifth Dynasty, which illustrate scenes from daily life and the seasons of the farming year, are among the most exquisite ever made. The discovery of furniture preserved in the tomb of Cheops' mother shows that crafts of this kind were equally accomplished. The armchair, bed, head rest, canopy, and caskets, sheathed

Graceful furniture from the tomb of Hetepheres, mother of Cheops, shows the elegant manner in which nobility of the Old Kingdom lived. This gold-covered bed and chair are inlaid with intricate designs. At the end of the bed is a head rest, the pillow of ancient Egyptians.

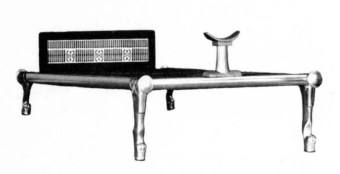

in gold and inlaid with faience, are of a superb simplicity of design. No queen's boudoir of any age was ever more elegantly furnished. Most people would agree that at least as far as sophisticated design was concerned, Egyptian culture was at its peak during the Old Kingdom.

After the Fourth Dynasty, the Pharaohs ceased to raise gigantic pyramids. Very much smaller tombs were built in the Fifth and Sixth Dynasties, a reflection of the declining stature of the kings. This was part of a more fundamental religious change. At Memphis, the creator god Horus had been supreme, but after the Fourth Dynasty the priests of the sun god Re at Heliopolis appear somehow to have gained an ascendancy over the throne. By now the Pharaohs were all entitled Son of Re, and their own divine powers seem to have diminished. Even in their portraits they are made to look more like ordinary human beings. Yet Egypt herself was still strong and enterprising. Expeditions were sent to the land of Punt (probably the Somali coast) to bring back incense and spices, and far south into Africa, from which they brought ivory, ebony, leopard skins, and living pygmies. Several campaigns were made against Asiatic fortresses, probably in Palestine, where according to Weni, a powerful governor from the south who organized and led the expeditions, they successfully crushed all resistance and brought back prisoners and booty.

During the Sixth Dynasty, however, the single authority of the Pharaoh and the central organization of government began to disintegrate. From the time of Narmer the whole land of Egypt had been recognized as belonging to the king. But in reign after reign, the Pharaoh had rewarded his chief officials (who were usually also members of his family) with titles and estates. At first these gifts were accepted as personal marks of favour given by Pharaoh, but in time they became hereditary, and their owners grew more lordly and independent. Soon, provincial governors could live like little Pharaohs; they no longer returned, as they had in the past, to be buried near the king, but had their tombs built at their own towns. The Pharaoh lost power, and revenue too, for many estates were exempt from taxation.

In about 2270 B.C., the Pharaoh Pepy II came to the throne as a child. He reigned about ninety years (the longest reign in all history), and when he died around the age of one hundred, the kingdom lapsed into anarchy. Thus the Old Kingdom, in which men had found that they

Pepy II, whose mother ruled during his childhood, sits on his mother's lap in this alabaster statuette.

could achieve almost unbelievable wonders, came to an end in misery.

The united kingdom of the two Egypts broke up into many parts, each dominated by competing rulers or warlords. Without any central government to resist them, wandering peoples such as Libyans from the west and Asiatics from the east, who had always taken refuge in Egypt at times of famine or danger, now came to stay, particularly in the delta. Foreign trade, upon which Egypt depended for all her wood, as well as for luxuries, broke down. At the same time, a social revolution seems to have taken place. Evidently the poor rose against hardship and injustice, and there followed the troubled century that historians now call the First Intermediate Period.

The self-confidence of the Old Kingdom, the certainty that under the divine Pharaoh and the other gods, order, justice, and prosperity would last for ever, had been destroyed and could never be fully restored. Although the country sustained great losses in prestige and power, and although her people were burdened with dreadful hardships, the decline of the old order did have a certain salutary effect. Men became more thoughtful as well as more sceptical and critical. Above all, a new social morality was born. Under the Old Kingdom young men had been advised to be sober, diligent, obedient to tradition and to their superiors, to the point of obsequiousness. Now they were encouraged to think of their souls and to be just and generous to the poor and helpless.

At last, in 2060 B.C., Mentuhotep II, a prince of Thebes in Upper Egypt, succeeded in crushing his chief rivals in Lower Egypt. He reunited the whole country during the Eleventh Dynasty, the beginning of the Middle Kingdom.

Writings that were inscribed during the Middle Kingdom seem to reflect a continuing development of the morality that had begun to stir the consciences of men at the end of the Old Kingdom. One text says, "Do not be evil, for kindliness is good. Make thy monument to be lasting through the love of thee." Another shows in memorable words how the deity is better pleased by goodness than by animal sacrifice: "More acceptable is the character of a just man than the ox of the evil doer." A third text describes how the supreme god made air and water for every man, adding, "I made every man like his fellow." That is to say, all men were born equal. Together with this new humanism went a new concept of the Pharaoh as the

As Egypt's arts and political system developed, her children still played old games. These Old Kingdom boys are merrily leapfrogging.

ORIENTAL INSTITUTE, UNIVERSITY OF CHICAGO

A scribe, usually pictured sitting cross-legged (above), was an official member of Egyptian society. The writing he used for documents is called hieratic; it was a kind of short-hand version of the hieroglyphic writing used for stone inscriptions. The inscription above at left shows several common hieroglyphs, including the ankh *sign (the first and last hieroglyphs), which stands for "life", and the large, painted eye, which expresses the word* an, *meaning "pleasant".*

good shepherd who cared for the well-being of his people.

During the few centuries of the Middle Kingdom, the rise and fall of the dynasties was perhaps less important than the cultural developments and the increasing contacts made with other nations. Under the Middle Kingdom, trade and commerce revived and increased—there was much traffic with Asia and with Crete. Egyptian power was again pushed southward into Nubia, and strong forts were built as far south as the Third Cataract to hold the conquered territory. As well as the flowering of literature, the visual arts returned to a kind of excellence, although they were quite different from the aristocratic, traditional forms of the Old Kingdom painting and sculpture. With the collapse of the Old Kingdom, Memphis had also declined as the centre of art, and many provincial schools of painting and sculpture arose. At the beginning of the Middle Kingdom, modest funerary decorations and carvings were made, often crudely drawn, but with vigour and freshness and a new interest in realistic details. At the royal court, which moved to Memphis at the beginning of the Twelfth Dynasty, great advances in technical skills appear in painted reliefs and sculptured hardstone statues of the Pharaohs.

During the Twelfth Dynasty, royal artists produced powerful portrait statues of the kings that show the new technical dexterity and the taste for realism that had be-

TEXT CONTINUED ON PAGE 32

THE MIDDLE KINGDOM:
BUSINESS AND BEAUTY

The two boats at left, from the tomb of a chancellor named Meket-Re, are models of the vessels he used on the Nile. Throughout the Middle Kingdom the artists who prepared works for dignitaries' tombs were commissioned to portray Egypt's river-based prosperity. The model in the background is a travelling boat, presumably made so that the dead chancellor's soul could enjoy the same luxury in the next world that he had in this one; bull-hide shields painted on the canopy were for defence against river pirates. On long trips, a kitchen tender, like the model in the foreground, accompanied him: on the deck, two ladies roll cakes of dough, a man pounds flour with a pestle, and another man stands in the bow to fend off. One source of Meket-Re's wealth is revealed in the model above of his granary. The seated scribes are shown tallying every grain, while slaves fetch and carry, and the overseer stands and watches. Artists of the Middle Kingdom also portrayed the natural beauty of their land and the ways of their people. The hippopotamuses at top on the opposite page are inscribed with lotuses. At top left on this page, in a relief carved in limestone, a noblewoman is having her hair dressed by a servant.

TEXT CONTINUED FROM PAGE 29

Though the Egyptians prided themselves as archers, the bows of the Hyksos were stronger. These Asiatic soldiers used a double-curved, or composite, bow (above) made of several layers of wood and horn.

gun to develop during the First Intermediate Period. The arts of the jeweller, during this time, reached a level of excellence and technical perfection that was never again achieved in Egyptian history.

Unfortunately, the relative order of the Middle Kingdom did not last very long. After the beginning of the Thirteenth Dynasty in 1786 B.C., the Pharaoh's central government again weakened and finally collapsed. There followed a century and a half of short, frequently interrupted reigns, probably with more than one dynasty in power at the same time. Then, near the end of this tumultuous period, called the Second Intermediate Period, around 1674 B.C., foreign kings ascended the throne. They were the Asiatic Hyksos, "Rulers of the Uplands", and they built a new capital, Avaris, in the delta. It used to be thought that the Hyksos had swept into Egypt from Asia as conquerors, but all archaeological evidence suggests that it was a process of infiltration. The biblical story of Joseph shows how semi-nomadic herdsmen came to Egypt from time to time, and how some were sold as slaves—or stayed on voluntarily as labourers. This had happened to some extent during the First Intermediate Period, and after the collapse of the Middle Kingdom, it had increased. As government authority weakened, the Asiatics had moved into the delta and had then struck successfully at Memphis itself.

Although Hyksos kings sat on the throne of the divine Pharaohs, they did not conquer all of Egypt's own land or that of her subjugated peoples. In Nubia there was a state half-Egyptian, half-African, under a prince of Kush. And most of Upper Egypt—from Asyut to the First Cataract—was still ruled by a Theban prince. His name was Sekenenra, and he was a man strong enough and confident enough to begin rallying his fellow Egyptians to drive out the Asiatic overlords.

Mounting an army, Sekenenra began a series of campaigns with the Hyksos which, upon his death in battle, were carried on with even greater success by his elder son, Kamose. It was this young and capable military leader who, by the beginning of the sixteenth century B.C. ultimately turned the tide of war against the foreigners—both for the liberation of his nation and to avenge his father.

A record exists of one of Kamose's expeditions against the Hyksos. Written in the first person, it describes how the king sailed down the Nile with his forces, encountered the enemy, and prepared to do battle with him the next day. "When the earth became light, I was on him as if it were a hawk . . . My soldiers were like lions with their prey . . . Your heart is undone, base Asiatic, who used to say 'I am lord, and there is none equal to me' . . ."

Like his father, Kamose is thought to have died in the campaign against the Hyksos, having enjoyed a comparatively brief reign. Fortunately for Egypt, however, this remarkable family of Theban princes had by no means exhausted its stock. Dominating the throne, particularly during the periods when her husband and older son were off on military campaigns was the remarkable queen mother, Ah-hotep. Now the queen sent forth from the palace another royal son, Ahmose, to expel the barbarians from their final stronghold.

The well-defended Hyksos capital withstood Ahmose's assaults and sieges for many years. But finally the efforts of the young Egyptian were crowned with victory. The Hyksos were driven from their remaining holdings in Lower Egypt, and Ahmose was recognized as the uncontested ruler of the land in 1570 B.C.

'Although the Egyptians of later periods looked back with horror on the time before the triumph of Ahmose, it did, in fact, bring lasting benefits. The Hyksos domination broke through the Egyptian love of tradition and the resistance to change, bringing the Nile valley increasingly in touch with the new ideas and techniques of the Asian cultures. The Hyksos rulers brought about the introduction of horses and fighting chariots, and with them the Asian type of composite bow, which could shoot much farther than the simple weapon used by the Egyptians. A stronger and more effective type of sword and dagger was also adopted, these now made of bronze. Among peaceful introductions were better weaving looms and a number of musical instruments—the lyre, the lute, the oboe, and the tambourine.

When Ahmose finally toppled the Hyksos régime and became king of both Upper and Lower Egypt, the great era of the New Kingdom began. During the next five hundred years Egypt's mightiest rulers extended the nation's borders to their farthest limits, raised magnificent and enormous monuments, and created a huge volume of literature as well as thousands of works of art, from colossal granite statues to exquisite ornaments of ivory and gold. The Egyptian empire achieved a brilliance surpassing even that of the Old Kingdom. It was also during this era that the Pharaohs themselves seemed nearest to the gods they chose to adore.

This ceremonial axe commemorates a victory over the Hyksos by Ahmose. The king, holding his foe by the hair, prepares to behead him.

II KINGS AND GODS

FPG: DUNCAN EDWARDS

The liberation of Egypt from the despised Hyksos and the restoration of a native ruler were carried out with energy and speed. When Ahmose was crowned in 1570 B.C., he chose his own city of Thebes to be the new capital of the kingdom, and he set up his palace there.

It was a royal capital unlike any the world had ever seen before—or would see again. Conditions in the Nile valley were such that Egypt never developed great cities of the size of those in Mesopotamia, where artisans, traders, and rich merchants were drawn together in pursuit of trade and commerce. Instead, Thebes was primarily a religious and ceremonial centre—a capital where the divine Pharaohs lived and where they built their principal

One of the many splendid temples at Thebes—the Pharaohs' capital on the east bank of the Nile—is in the foreground of this view. In the cliffs across the river are the tombs of New Kingdom Pharaohs.

temples. Surrounding these palaces and temples were residential areas, for the Pharaohs had to be served by a host of priests, officials, scribes, and soldiers. These, in their turn, attracted thousands of humbler people to serve their needs.

Thebes, which was to become the richest and most powerful city of the ancient world, had a setting worthy of its grandeur. Here, the strip of fertile soil on the east bank of the Nile widened, and there was a broad expanse of pasture, cornfields and orchards, fine groves of date palms, and an abundance of vegetables to feed the people of the new capital. It was on the eastern bank of the Nile that the centre of the town was to grow, and with it the two main groups of temples, one at Karnak, the other at Luxor, the two being linked by a magnificent ceremonial way.

On the western side of the Nile, beyond the strip of cultivated land, the desert rose rapidly by rocky slopes and precipices to the pointed summit now called El Qurn. There, in western Thebes, the presence of the Pharaoh dominated the city. There, a succession of kings built their funerary temples, their palaces and pleasure gardens, while

Seated on a bronze throne, the goddess Isis is shown in the statuette at right with her protective wings at rest and her son Horus on her lap. Among her many duties and functions was to care for the Pharaohs' throne.

in the background were the harsh valleys that harboured the royal tombs.

Even though the Nile widens at Thebes, the buildings on one side could still be seen from those on the other side, and there was a regular stream of little boats to and fro, carrying passengers and goods from one part of the town to the other. Occasionally, with greater pomp, there were barges hurrying priests and officials—even the high priest and the vizier—about their business. From time to time, the Pharaoh himself sailed across in state as he went from his palace to play his role in the temple rites at Karnak and Luxor.

The title "Pharaoh" is derived from the Egyptian *per aa*, which simply meant "great house", and was one of the ways of referring to the royal palace. It does not seem to have been used to refer to the king himself until the time of the New Kingdom. The Hebrew authors of the Bible used the term "Pharaoh" to refer to any reigning king of Egypt, and the word has come down into modern language from this source.

The Pharaohs of the New Kingdom inherited one of the oldest continuous monarchies the world has ever known. Although it had been interrupted twice by social upheavals and foreign interference, the effects of these events were only temporary. When Ahmose won the throne and Egypt was reunited, the traditional ways were resumed once more.

The course of the Pharaoh's days and years was marked by daily rites and festivals in the various cities, in which he frequently played a leading role. In addition, each reign had its own ritual occasions, from the accession and coronation celebrations through the *Sed* festival, or jubilee, to the death rites.

How, first of all, was it determined who should succeed to the throne? As a rule, the Pharaoh's eldest son by his principal queen, or great wife, was his heir. If the great wife failed to provide a son, the child of a secondary wife could become the crown prince. The royal heiress, that is, the Pharaoh's eldest daughter by his great wife, was also important to the succession. Although she could not rule, marriage to her could strengthen a prince's claim to the throne. (During some periods of Egyptian history, the inheritance went through the female line, and the right to the succession was vested in the person of the royal heiress, but that was the exception rather than the rule.) For this reason, and because of the belief that the divine

blood of royalty should not be diluted, the new Pharaoh often took as his great wife his sister or his half-sister. And occasionally, if there was no other eligible royal heiress, the Pharaoh married his own daughter (see dynastic chart on page 56).

In addition to his great wife and his secondary wives (who, by New Kingdom times, were often the daughters of foreign kings, married for political reasons), there were also numbers of concubines. These ladies lived together in the harem, which was an important part of the palace. If there was no other eligible heir, even the son of a concubine might be chosen as a successor to the throne.

This, then, was the theory of the succession, but it quite often broke down in the face of human pressures. A man or woman of strong personality would insist on getting his or her own way. Several times a Pharaoh took a woman who was not a royal heiress as his great wife, and twice in the long history of Egypt, a woman succeeded in getting herself recognized as the Pharaoh.

For Egypt to have been without a Pharaoh would have been disastrous, so the accession ceremonies took place immediately after the death of the old ruler. (On some occasions the heir was even appointed as co-regent long before the king's death as happened in the Nineteenth Dynasty, in the reign of Amenmeses, when for a time there were two Pharaohs on the throne at the same time.) The heir was presented to the ancestral gods in their shrines and then to "the nobles of the king, the notables, the friends, the courtiers, and the chiefs of the people". Finally, before a large crowd, the five sacred titles chosen for the new Pharaoh were proclaimed, and there was great rejoicing. The whole accession ceremony expressed the idea of "The king is dead! Long live the king!"

There was now an interval before the coronation itself could be celebrated. One reason for this was that the new king could not be crowned until the old one was buried, and the embalming of the royal corpse took at least seventy days. Another cause of delay was that the coronation had to be held on New Year's Day or on one of the other festivals of renewal. This was to emphasize the idea, important

In the wall painting opposite, the Pharaoh offers libations to Osiris, who holds the crook and flail, symbols of kingly power. Two other symbols that figured in the Pharaoh's accession ceremonies were the lotus and papyrus insignia of Upper and Lower Egypt, which are visible on the pillars above.

to the Egyptians, that a new reign meant a fresh beginning —a rebirth of the kingdom. In the archives of the kings even the royal hierarchal calendar was made to mark a new reign with the Year I (a system that has been a source of much difficulty for archaeologists), although a regular calendar based on twelve months had been in use since the earliest dynasties of the Old Kingdom.

The coronation was held in the capital city, which, during most of the New Kingdom, was Thebes. It involved a great many religious rites, and the high priests of the various gods formally presented the crowns—identical to those with which Narmer was installed on the throne over sixteen hundred years before—to the king. The Pharaoh probably went first to a shrine decorated with the lotus (blue water-lily), an emblem of Upper Egypt, and there briefly donned the White Crown, a high, conical hat with a bulbous tip. He then turned to a second shrine embellished with the papyrus reed of Lower Egypt; there he put on the Red Crown, a flat-topped headdress with a projecting shaft at the back and a metal coil in the front.

The double coronation was one example of the duality of thought that ran through royal and religious observances, and through civil life as well. One of its central manifestations was in the idea of the double kingdom. Although this concept had some historical and geographical justification, it was enormously magnified in the official ceremonies and observances. The king was always known as the Lord of the Two Lands, and in many rituals besides that of the coronation, he had to duplicate his ceremonial acts in the name of both Upper and Lower Egypt.

During the coronation itself, the king put on many other crowns, each of which had its own meaning and was appropriate to a particular occasion. One was the handsome Blue Crown, or helmet, of the warrior king. All the crowns concealed the Pharaoh's most sacred hair, and never again would he appear in public with a single strand showing.

In addition to the many crowns he had to place on his head, the king was vested in a cape and sacred jewels. Then, in a solemn climax, the Pharaoh received two sceptres in the form of the golden crook and the flail, emblems of Osiris. Now indeed he was Lord of the Two Lands.

The Pharaoh had not been silent during these rites; he addressed the gods and goddesses present in the insignia, taking unto himself their divine power. Thus he said, "Let there be terror of me like the terror of thee. Let

Each crown the Pharaoh wore represented a different part of his kingship. The White Crown (top) symbolized Upper Egypt, the Red Crown (centre) was the emblem of Lower Egypt, and the combination of these two, the Double Crown (bottom), signified the unification of the Two Lands of Egypt.

there be awe of me like the awe of thee. Let there be love of me like the love of thee."

Another part of the coronation ceremony was called the Circuit of the Walls. This had originated in Memphis, when the early kings actually paced around the city. In the New Kingdom, the ceremonial walk had probably been reduced to a symbolic rite expressing the idea of the Pharaoh as "Lord of All That The Sun Encircles".

The coronation was an occasion of great popular celebration. People had been crowding into Thebes for many days, on foot or in small sailing and rowing boats. The city was full to bursting, with people sleeping on all the roofs and in the streets. The populace was not, of course, admitted to the actual coronation in the temple, but there was much else to entertain them. The day before, they would have seen some part of the burial of the old king, and there was the arrival of goods and notables by ship, and processions in the streets. There was also a distribution of food and clothes to the poor, and much wine and beer was drunk.

The other great ritual of the king's life was the *Sed* festival. The central purpose of the festival was the revitalization of the Pharaoh—a reaffirmation of faith in him and his régime. It ensured that his powers were restored, that he was brought into harmony with nature and the gods, thus maintaining the well-being of his people. The festival was held on an anniversary of the coronation, but it could be celebrated more than once, and the number of years it marked might vary widely. Some Pharaohs held their first *Sed* early in their reign, while others waited for as many as thirty years. The festival lasted for several days and involved a large number of processions, enthronements, and visits by the king to the shrines of the gods. Leading subjects paid homage to the king at this time, and there were also symbolic enactments such as the king crossing a field that represented the land of Egypt, the washing of feet, and, at the end, the shooting of arrows to the four points of the compass. Here again, most rites were enacted twice for the sake of the two lands. The queen and all the royal children and kinsmen took part, and the populace was more closely involved than at the actual coronation.

While the *Sed* festival occurred only a few times during a Pharaoh's reign, a number of other ceremonial occasions took place throughout the year. There were the small daily rites such as the prayer to the rising sun. Then

The Blue Crown, or casque (above), was worn by the Pharaoh in battle or when he wished to emphasize his military feats and warlike powers.

In battle, the armies of the Pharaohs often fought Egypt's ancient foes the Syrians and the Nubians. The decorative tiles on these two pages depict a bearded Syrian soldier (above) and a Nubian captive (opposite). Both tiles were made for a Nineteenth Dynasty palace.

there were the many annual festivals linked with the cycle of the seasons and with the celebrations of different gods.

Pharaohs of the New Kingdom, for example, certainly took part in the festival of Amon, the god of Thebes. And as the king was expected to travel up and down the Nile bringing his divine presence to as many of his subjects as possible, he took part in the more important provincial festivals. One of the greatest of these was the festival of Osiris at Abydos. This took the form of a mystery play enacting the life, death, and resurrection of the god. It drew thousands of worshippers to the city where, traditionally, the king of the hereafter was buried.

In practical matters, the duties and responsibilities of the Pharaoh somewhat resembled those of modern rulers and can be divided roughly into administrative, military, and judicial functions. However, such functions were not entirely separated from the sacred and theological aspect of the king's role. For as a divine figure, everything the Pharaoh did had religious significance and was likely to be accompanied by prayers, offerings, or other rites.

The amount of administrative business that was dealt with in Thebes at the height of the empire was enormous— and much of it passed through the king's hands. The Pharaoh usually had a session in the morning with the vizier and the treasurer. They had to hear endless reports and appeals from officials such as the governors of the nomes, perhaps concerning plans for irrigation and other public works. They had to consider news of riots and other disasters, questions of taxation, the management of the army, and appointments to high office. From kings and embassies abroad they also received diplomatic dispatches that they had to read and assess. The hundreds of inscribed clay tablets discovered in the royal archives at Tell el Amarna (page 145) have revealed that a considerable correspondence of this kind was maintained with the kings and the princes of western Asia.

The Pharaoh's military responsibilities were also very heavy. They increased during Middle Kingdom times when civil order and a reunited central government had finally been established by armed force. In the New Kingdom, the extension of the empire and the wars against neighbouring states made the king's role as the supreme warrior one of great importance. Throughout history, kings have usually been called the commanders-in-chief of their military forces, but they have not been expected to lead their armies in person. This honorary status was some-

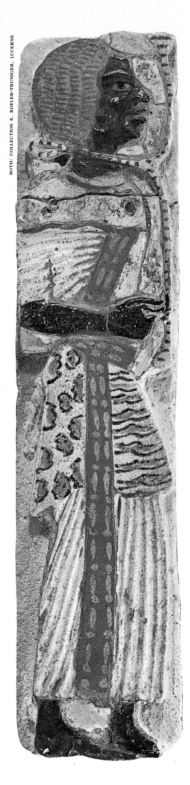

times granted in Egypt: an official inscription may claim that the king led his forces to victory, when in fact he was safely at home. It probably would not be correct to assume that all the stirring pictures in which the Pharaoh is shown trampling crowds of Nubians or Semites below the hoofs of his chariot horses are entirely accurate. But it is known from the records of Tuthmosis III and Ramesses II that the Pharaohs did lead some campaigns and did take part in the actual fighting.

One of the most important of all the royal functions was to mete out justice. While the Pharaoh's power over his subjects was absolute, it was never intended to be arbitrary. It was his obligation to maintain a state of perfect order for all his people. The king was supposed to exemplify *maat*, a word best translated as "rightness", or "truth and justice". *Maat* was personified as a beautiful goddess, daughter of the sun god Re, and is often shown in coronation scenes accompanying the Pharaoh.

Being both the maker of all the laws and the final judge in all disputes involved a good deal of hard work for the Pharaoh. He was the only one who could hand down the death sentence and the only one who could commute it, and even in lesser matters, any of his subjects might appeal to him for justice. However, very few petitioners actually reached the royal presence. The office of the vizier, who was called Steward of the Whole Land and Counsellor of All Orders of the King, dealt with all but the most important or difficult cases. All cases, however, were regularly submitted to the Pharaoh for final judgment.

The fact that the Pharaoh's judicial responsibilities were symbolized in the person of a goddess, whose name often appeared among the king's sacred titles, is one indication of the close relationship between the practical and religious aspects of the kingship.

The theology of Egyptian kingship sounds complicated, but its overall meaning is simple. The Pharaoh belonged both to the world of the gods and the world of men, and he was seen as a bridge between them. Some of the local deities represented various aspects of nature, such as the earth and the sky or the Nile and its gift of fertility. So the king, living in their midst, could bring the Egyptians into a harmonious relationship with their divinities and with the forces of nature upon which their whole existence depended.

The common man in Egypt, living as he did in a land of sharp contrasts, the fertile valley and the arid desert, conceived of both his physical and his spiritual world as a perfectly balanced combination of opposites, while regularity and order in nature were at the heart of his existence. Changes were seasonal and rhythmic rather than progressive, and this view of his material world was also reflected in his spiritual life. The Egyptian had no sense of guilt nor a belief in original sin, as in Christian theology. While he believed that man could transgress, he also believed that the gods would punish him and then forgive his sins. The important thing was for men to live in harmony with *maat*, and a peaceful, contented, harmonious way of life was to be desired above all things.

The Pharaoh himself was accepted by the Egyptians as a god incarnate during Old Kingdom times, and by the time of the New Kingdom, as the descendant of the chief god. Throughout history, many rulers have been believed by their subjects to be the divinely chosen stewards of the gods, and the idea of divine right by which kings rule is still a familiar one. But with the Pharaoh it was different: he was no mere servant or delegate of divinity; he was, as the vizier of Tuthmosis III said, "the god by whose guidance men live".

The Pharaoh was identified with most of the gods of the Egyptian pantheon according to the occasion and the place. If he took part in the festival of the god of one of the nomes, he was believed to represent that local god. But always and everywhere, he was identified with three of the greatest of the national divinities: Horus, Osiris, and Re.

As a living king, the Pharaoh was Horus; for the ordinary Egyptian man or woman, this was the most important

The officials of the Pharaoh were generally strict—and occasionally severe. In the relief below, one farmer is about to be whipped for tax delinquency; others kneel as a scribe records their depositions.

A prosperous Pharaonic official of the Nineteenth Dynasty was Apuy, whose house is shown in this wall painting. A slave waters the verdant garden by means of a shaduf, a bucket suspended from a weighted beam that swings on a raised pivot.

meaning of the divinity of their king. In a detail on the Narmer palette the king appears as Horus the Falcon—a sky god often shown with the sun disc on his head. This belief that the Pharaoh was Horus incarnate persisted throughout the Old Kingdom. By the end of that period, the king's place in the Horus mythology had shifted slightly. Horus was the son of the god Osiris and the goddess Isis. Osiris had been killed and then dismembered by the fierce god Seth but was made whole and brought back to life by his wife Isis. The goddess then conceived and bore their son Horus, who avenged his father by fighting Seth. Horus was victorious, but in the struggle he lost his eye, and this eye became a symbol to Egyptians for all sacrifices that sons made for their fathers. Though the Pharaoh was the good Horus, he was also seen to reconcile the opposites of good and evil in his own divine person, and in this sense, he was Horus-with-Seth.

As for Osiris, as his part in the myth shows, he was a god of renewed life, of resurrection, in the Nile and its

45

flood, in the seed corn, and in man. His worshippers believed that he granted eternal life, and because of this he became also the recognized god of the dead and judge of souls.

The Pharaoh shared in these powers and is often shown in the likeness of Osiris. In this way, the king could assure the continued succession of his family dynasty. For just as the living Pharaoh was Horus, in death he became Osiris, and his heir was reborn as Horus. Thus the immortality of the kingship, if not of the king, was ensured for ever.

During the Old Kingdom, the throne also came under the influence of the cult of Re, the sun god, whose centre was at Heliopolis. According to the legend, Re created the world by rising in the heavens on the "primeval hill"— the spot where land first emerged above the chaos of water. Therefore he became the mythical first king of Egypt, and every Pharaoh was seen as inheriting the throne as a son of Re.

When the vigorous princes of Thebes took over the kingship, the Theban gods too became supreme. In the new capital city, the god Amon was the chief deity, and the largest of the Theban temples were dedicated to him. However, in the New Kingdom, the Pharaoh was still seen as the son of Re, and to unite the two traditions, Amon, whose name means "the Hidden One", became Amon-Re, king of the gods and the supreme deity of Egypt.

In the Egyptian pantheon there were different sets of gods for Upper and Lower Egypt. Such duplication was evident, for example, in the deities associated with the White and Red Crowns. Nekhbet, the vulture goddess of Upper Egypt, was felt to be present in the White Crown, and Wazet, the cobra goddess of Lower Egypt, in the Red Crown. The symbol of the cobra was always worn by the Pharaoh on his brow and was perhaps the most significant of all the royal insignia. The snake was imagined metaphorically as protecting the king by spitting at his foes. The vulture was also protective and was often shown with wings outstretched above the king's head. Occasionally (as on the funerary mask of King Tutankhamon) its emblem was beside the serpent on the royal forehead.

When not in their serpent and bird forms, Wazet and Nekhbet were portrayed as young women, with idealized features, attending the Pharaoh. They were referred to rather charmingly among the royal inscriptions as "the Two Ladies".

The kingship of Egypt was not only extraordinarily old;

On the forehead of Pharaoh Tutankhamon's funerary mask are the animal goddesses of Upper and Lower Egypt: the vulture Nekhbet (at left) and the cobra Wazet.

it was also a matter of incredible significance to all the Egyptian people. Anyone who has seen the great monuments and works of art of ancient Egypt would have little difficulty in believing this, for the temples were dominated by colossal statues of the Pharaoh, and the vast walls were covered with painted reliefs showing scenes of the Pharaoh's life and death. In such representations, the king is always shown much larger than the ordinary mortals around him. Egyptian artists worked according to fairly rigid conventions, one of which was that human figures should be scaled according to their relative importance. Thus, on the walls of his temples, the Pharaoh is shown in heroic proportions, trampling his smaller-scaled enemies.

In murals, the Pharaoh is sometimes depicted holding conquered enemy princes by their hair, and sometimes he is galloping his chariot into battle or off on a wild-beast hunt. Most often, he is portrayed taking his place as an equal among the divinities of Egypt—standing face to face with Amon-Re, king of the gods, or with his hand being held by Isis, the supreme goddess.

These scenes, the colossal statues, and the labour and treasure that were lavished on the rock-cut royal tombs, all reveal the exalted status of the Egyptian kingship. Sovereigns have often been rich and powerful and highly venerated by their subjects, but there has rarely been anything to equal the total supremacy of the Pharaohs.

However many *Sed* festivals he had held, the Pharaoh at last had to die. Full preparations had been made during his lifetime, the king himself supervising the building of his tomb. In the New Kingdom the building of pyramids had been given up, largely because it had proved impossible to prevent robbers from ransacking the treasure-filled chambers. A man called Enene, architect of Tuthmosis I, originated the idea of concealing the royal burial places. He recorded how he "witnessed the hewing out of the rock tomb of His Majesty in the solitary place where nobody could look on, and where nobody could listen". This "solitary place" is a valley running up into the craggy mountains immediately to the west of Thebes—now known as the Valley of the Kings. The Valley of the Queens is in another valley a mile or so to the south-west, and a great many of the nobles and high officials of the New Kingdom were buried on the intervening slopes.

Passages and large halls were hacked out of the limestone cliffs and were decorated with hundreds of scenes

Many times larger than the little queen who stands by his knee, the Pharaoh portrayed above (Ramesses II) is a study in royal supremacy.

TEXT CONTINUED ON PAGE 50

PREPARING FOR THE AFTER-LIFE

When the god Osiris suffered and died at the hands of his brother Seth, his dismembered body was recovered by Isis, his wife, who resurrected him. Osiris became king of the dead. From this story stems the Egyptians' belief in the desirability of preparing the dead for the after-life; and although the first Pharaohs were probably buried with just a few necessities for the next world, burials rapidly became more elaborate. The most gigantic Pharaonic tomb is the pyramid of Cheops, which stands 485 feet high and covers 13 acres. Although none of his successors' resting places were as imposing from the outside, each was a storehouse of treasure for life in the next world. Corpses of kings and other dignitaries were mummified, with the idea that the spirits would return and would need their bodies. First the bodies were stripped of internal organs and fatty tissue; then they were dried out with absorbent powders and aromatics. Once the body was free of moisture, the attending priests covered it with golden rings, pendants, amulets, and charms in order to transfer the incorruptibility of gold to the body of the dead man. When the priests began the process of wrapping, they used long strips of linen, adding more pieces of

gold and a scarab to represent the dead man's heart. Finally they covered the body with a layer of linen treated with another preservative unguent, which had the effect of darkening, and drying, the skin. By the end of the mummification process, bodies were little more than well-dressed shells of hardened skin, bones, and cartilage. The mummies were laid out in handsomely decorated wooden cases, like the ones in the frieze above. The bodies of the sculptors Ipuky and Nebamun are contained in these cases, and each is attended to by a priest; purifying waters are sprinkled on the coffins, and one of the widows heaps dust on her head. She has bared her breast in remorse, and she lays her hand at the foot of her husband's coffin. After a procession characterized by wailing, dancing, and prayers, and attended by priests, relatives, and professional mourners, the mummy was taken inside the tomb. It was laid with food, clothing, equipment, and treasure in a sarcophagus like the one opposite, above, inscribed with pictures of Horus' eyes (at centre), various gods, and Isis (at the end). The wall painting below it shows the dog-headed god Anubis preparing a dead man to have his heart scarab weighed in the presence of Osiris.

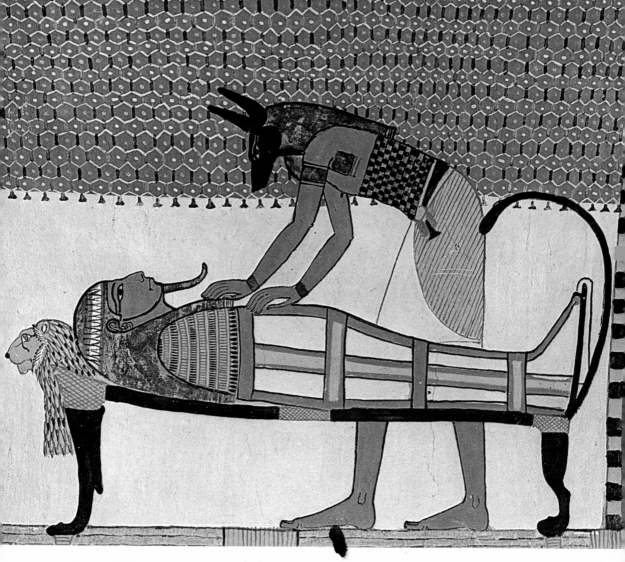

TEXT CONTINUED FROM PAGE 47

and long hieroglyphic texts designed to help the king on his difficult and dangerous journey to eternity. The scenes in the entrance passage show the Pharaoh being reunited with Re, but in the depth of the inner chambers are the strange realms and monsters of the afterworld kingdom of Osiris. Unlike the tombs of ordinary mortals, which were decorated with delightful pictures of everyday life, the burial place of the Pharaoh was a solemn and forbidding chamber.

Furniture, wagons, clothing, weapons, and equipment of all kinds were also placed in the tomb, for it was felt that material comforts would be needed in the afterworld

One of the best preserved and most decorative of the tombs found in western Thebes is seen below. The wall paintings depict life in the "Garden of Ialu", the Egyptian paradise. At the top, the sun god is worshipped by two dog-headed apes.

FPG: DUNCAN EDWARD

just as they had been during the king's lifetime. The discovery of the tomb of Tutankhamon (see pages 142–143), the only royal grave to have been found really intact, shows how amazingly abundant and splendid the burial objects were. The making of such funerary treasures required tens of thousands of hours of work on the part of the finest artists and craftsmen.

As soon as the king died his body was hurried away to the slabs and tanks of the embalmers, who worked under the protection of the jackal god, Anubis. The body was pickled in natron and rubbed with sweet oils and aromatics, and the internal organs were taken out and put into the handsomely carved large containers, called canopic jars, made for that purpose. When the corpse had been made durable it was bandaged in linen, supplied with scarabs and all manner of amulets and spells, decked with splendid jewels, and then enclosed in a series of magnificent coffins—the innermost perhaps of pure gold.

While mummification was going on, the Egyptians believed that the individual was neither alive nor dead. His *ka*, or vital energy, was at rest, awaiting his arrival in the afterworld, a reunion that could not take place until the rites of the funeral had been celebrated. The king's *ka* was shown as a kind of twin to the monarch himself; those of commoners were never shown at all. It was understood that they were all derived from the royal *ka*, for it was the king who gave to every man his vital force.

One can imagine the tremendous funeral ceremonies and scenes that took place as the royal mummy was borne across the Nile and through the fields, then up among the crags to the place where the open gateway led into the rock. There were bands of mourning women, their hair hanging down, beating their foreheads and wailing. There was the long cortège of the royal kinsmen, the nobles and priests, a mass of precious furniture, effigies bright with gold, great baskets of food and drink, and lines of animals for sacrifice. This was the time of the festival of Osiris, with whom the dead king was to be made one. Everyone was confident that the Pharaoh would enter the boat of the sun god, sail with him through the gates of the west into the afterworld, and then, having triumphed over the powers of darkness, rise again to eternal life as surely as his father Re would rise in the east. And, walled into the mountain though he was, the king was not lost to his people. As a divine ancestor, he would help them in this world, and as Osiris, he would improve their chances in the next.

These typical funerary objects of the New Kingdom were found in tombs of different dynasties: the statuette of a servant (top) dates from the Eighteenth Dynasty; the ape-headed canopic jar (which contains the stomach of the deceased) lates from the Nineteenth Dynasty.

III

BUILDERS OF EMPIRE

In the New Kingdom, Thebes became richer and more important than ever as the empire-building ambitions of the Pharaohs grew. When the armies of Ahmose pursued the defeated Hyksos rulers into Palestine, the intention had probably been only to secure Egypt against further threat from Asia. But in time, policy became more positively aggressive; Pharaohs boasted of their campaigns "to extend the frontiers of Egypt". They were in a strong position to do so, for the liberation of their country had left them with a well-trained army, jubilant after its victories, equipped with superior types of weapons taken over from the Asiatics (see page 32), and above all, experienced now in the use of the war chariot. The chariot was drawn by a pair of powerful horses, and attached to the side of each vehicle was a large quiver of arrows. When the Egyptians raced the chariots into crowds of foot soldiers while shooting volleys of arrows from their composite bows, they must have spread terror in their wake. And behind all this display of military might was the growing spirit of nationalism —a patriotic fervour that had scarcely before existed in Egypt.

Thus, in the New Kingdom during the early days, the Pharaohs were involved in aggressive wars to dominate the neighbouring peoples. Occasionally they fought with the Libyans from the Western Desert, but more often they were embroiled with the Nubians to the south and with the various shifting Asiatic peoples to the north-east.

Nubia was relatively easy to manage. In spite of the rough and dangerous waters around the cataracts, it could be reached up the river, and the Nubians, having a less

Under Tuthmosis III, the Egyptian empire reached its fullest extent. In the wall painting opposite, he holds an incense bowl as he pours a libation to his divine patron, Amon-Re. Above are royal spear- and shield-bearers.

53

dominant culture, soon adapted an Egyptian style and manner. The Nubian countryside was fortified with strongholds and new cities were built. From Nubia the Egyptians brought out copper, gold, amethyst, and other semiprecious stones from the mines and quarries, and took ivory and spotted cattle from the plains. To represent them in Nubia, the Eighteenth Dynasty Pharaohs appointed a regent who was known as the King's Son and Overseer of the Southern Countries. There were uprisings from time to time, but Egypt held fast and always put down the rebellions.

The situation in Palestine and Syria, which Egypt regarded as her western Asian territories, was more difficult, for the Egyptians had to travel over deserts and seas to reach them. Beyond Palestine and Syria were the great powers who challenged Egypt's bid for supremacy—the Assyrians, the Mitanni, and the Hittites, all pressing westward from Asia (see map on page 57).

National boundaries were vague: Palestine and Syria each comprised a number of loose federations of small city-states. In these city-states lived a hodge-podge of Canaanites, Amorites, Phoenicians, and other peoples who constantly quarrelled among themselves and were always ready to fight. They made and broke alliances with their more powerful neighbours and generally created an unstable, fractious region. Adding to the instability were the Sa Gaz, a people living in the hills and forests who engaged in guerrilla warfare, occasionally serving as mercenaries for one group or another.

Egypt's determination to dominate such a turbulent region presented obvious difficulties and dangers. At first most of the petty kings were quite ready to recognize the revived strength of Egypt and to pay tribute to the Pharaoh. In the south, Ahmose's son, Amenhotep I, who had succeeded to his father's throne, devoted most of his energies to strengthening Egypt's control over Nubia. In 1525 B.C., he was followed by a more ambitious Pharaoh whose claim to the throne rested on his marriage into the royal family. This was Tuthmosis I.

Early in his reign Tuthmosis sailed far up the Nile with Ahmose, an admiral who had served under two previous Pharaohs. Ahmose relates how he carefully navigated the rough waters of the Third Cataract while Tuthmosis was "raging like a panther". He describes in grisly detail how the king killed a Nubian chieftain with an arrow and hung his body from the prow of the ship. The

In a detail from a funerary chest, Egyptian soldiers (in white tunics) are depicted unleashing a fierce attack on the hapless Syrians. Despite their advantage in numbers and in war chariots, the Asiatic defenders were no match for the aggressive and well-disciplined warriors of the Pharaoh.

55

wars of the Pharaohs were conducted with savage brutality. Reliefs carved on the walls of temples in Thebes show great piles of human hands—cut from defeated enemies. Again and again Pharaohs are shown holding prisoners by the hair and preparing to crush in their skulls with the heavy royal mace. This could be a mere symbol of conquest, but it seems that kings of Egypt did in fact dispatch enemy leaders in this way.

The Nubian foray was followed by a remarkable military feat. Tuthmosis led his army thirteen hundred miles from Thebes into Syria, all the way to the River Euphrates. Crossing the river, he defeated the Mitanni, who had come into Mesopotamia as conquerors from the north. Then, far from his Theban palace, the king, with justifiable pride, erected a stone stela (marker) commemorating his victorious campaign, in which he claimed to have slaugh-

The inbred and complex line of succession to the Pharaoh's throne in the Eighteenth Dynasty is traced by following the light and dark lines on this simplified chart.

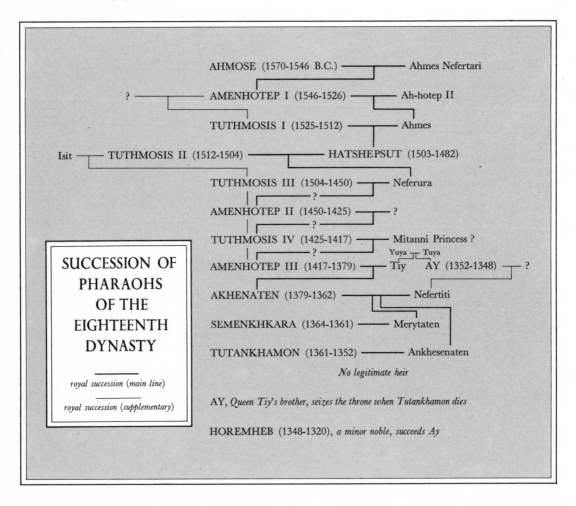

SUCCESSION OF PHARAOHS OF THE EIGHTEENTH DYNASTY

——— *royal succession (main line)*

——— *royal succession (supplementary)*

AHMOSE (1570-1546 B.C.) ——— Ahmes Nefertari

? ——— AMENHOTEP I (1546-1526) ——— Ah-hotep II

TUTHMOSIS I (1525-1512) ——— Ahmes

Isit ——— TUTHMOSIS II (1512-1504) ——— HATSHEPSUT (1503-1482)

TUTHMOSIS III (1504-1450) ——— Neferura

? ———

AMENHOTEP II (1450-1425) ——— ?

? ———

TUTHMOSIS IV (1425-1417) ——— Mitanni Princess ?

? ———   Yuya ┬┬ Tuya

AMENHOTEP III (1417-1379) ——— Tiy   AY (1352-1348) ——┬ ?

AKHENATEN (1379-1362) ——— Nefertiti

SEMENKHKARA (1364-1361) ——— Merytaten

TUTANKHAMON (1361-1352) ——— Ankhesenaten

No legitimate heir

AY, *Queen Tiy's brother, seizes the throne when Tutankhamon dies*

HOREMHEB (1348-1320), *a minor noble, succeeds Ay*

tered great numbers of the enemy and to have carried off many more prisoners.

Only one other Pharaoh, Tuthmosis' grandson and the third of the name, ever penetrated so far into hostile Asia. He found his grandfather's memorial still standing, and he must have read its message with admiration before raising his own stela beside it.

With conquests such as these, foreign tribute flowed into Thebes, and Tuthmosis I spent some of it in adding new buildings and works of art to the great temples beside the Nile. When he died, he was the first Pharaoh to be buried in the Valley of the Kings.

By his great wife, the royal heiress Ahmes, Tuthmosis I had a daughter whose name was Hatshepsut. By a lesser wife, he had a son, Tuthmosis. The young heir married his half-sister (a frequent occurrence among Egyptian royalty),

Tuthmosis III's conquests (shaded on this map) took his armies to the Euphrates. Most of his successors were content with tribute-raising expeditions to the south.

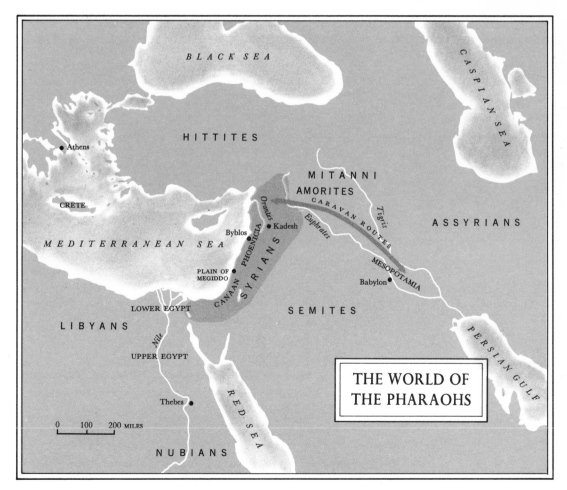

In the peaceful reign of Hatshep-
sut, foreigners continued to render
homage to the Pharaoh. Here, a
Nubian (wearing ostrich plumes)
and a Syrian kneel before the throne.

and on the old king's death in about 1512 B.C., his son succeeded him as Tuthmosis II. Hatshepsut, now "King's Daughter, King's Sister, God's Wife, and King's Great Wife", was evidently a woman of strong and vivid personality. It may be that she was inclined to overshadow her half-brother and husband. Certainly not very much is known of his reign except that he had to put down a revolt in Nubia and that he also fought in Palestine. Tuthmosis II and Hatshepsut had no sons, and when Tuthmosis died, the most suitable male heir was a boy born to him by a concubine named Isit. He was crowned, but until the day Hatshepsut died, the young king had to contend with his formidable and talented stepmother-aunt.

At first Hatshepsut acted as regent to the young king, who had ascended the throne as the third Tuthmosis. But Hatshepsut had been close to the throne all her life, and she felt that she had royal power as well as the purest royal blood in her veins. After a few years she herself assumed the Double Crown. Tuthmosis III was still recognized as co-ruler, but he receded into the background.

It was an unprecedented situation, and there were immediate practical difficulties. For example, all the royal titles were in masculine form, and the inscription cutters had to adapt them, sometimes making mistakes. Then in the many sculptured portraits, Hatshepsut sometimes had herself shown breastless and in man's dress—including the artificial beard that Egyptian kings often wore—and sometimes with a shapely figure and in a woman's dress. Despite the many problems in Hatshepsut's official and ceremonial life, her reign was undeniably prosperous and successful.

Since she could not lead armies of soldiers, she kept the peace and (like Elizabeth I of England and other great queens) was able to accumulate wealth for many constructive enterprises. The vizier Hapu-seneb, who was also High Priest of Amon, was a political power behind her throne; but evidently far closer to her was an arrogant, self-made man named Senmut.

Senmut was exceedingly presumptuous—he acquired no less than eighty official titles and had memorials and a tomb made for himself in the queen's funerary temple, where no mere mortal had any right to show his name. But apparently Hatshepsut loved him, and undoubtedly he had ability. Hatshepsut repaired many temples throughout the land, which had been in ruinous condition since Hyksos days, and she also added some buildings and two magnificent obelisks to the temple complex at Karnak.

Her noblest architectural achievement was the funerary temple at Deir el Bahri, opposite Karnak, which she commissioned Senmut to build for her. With imaginative boldness, they chose the site on the cliff of El Qurn, a natural semicircle separated from the Valley of the Kings by no more than a spine of rock. The walls of the temple are precipitous and are beautifully banded in shades of soft pink and buff stone. There was one old building on this site already, the tomb of the King Mentuhotep, who had redeemed Egypt five centuries before. Senmut set Hatshepsut's temple higher up and made it much larger, but he harmonized the styles, creating a simple, colonnaded façade (see overleaf).

To modern eyes Hatshepsut's temple at Deir el Bahri is indeed one of the most beautiful buildings in Thebes, and even in all Egypt. It is built on two vast, shallow terraces rising up to meet the foot of the precipice. It is approached along an avenue, originally flanked by sphinxes, which leads into a courtyard planted with vines and palm trees. Both this court and the terrace above it provide a beautiful base for the splendid group of buildings on the second terrace. Along the front of this terrace is a long portico that once held twenty-six colossal statues of the queen in the likeness of Osiris. Behind the portico are a great pillared hall, sanctuaries, and the royal funerary chapel. The buildings are all a golden-white limestone, which glistens against the mountain crags that hang above them like a canopy. The innermost sanctuary, the most holy of holies, is carved into this native rock.

Deir el Bahri, dedicated to the memory of Hatshepsut, but with sanctuaries also for the goddess Hathor (in the form of a cow), the god Anubis, and the sun god Re, is not only a work of art in itself but houses many remarkable reliefs. The most interesting of these are scenes which illustrate ships bringing two huge obelisks down river from the isle of Elephantine, near Aswan. The queen had four of these lofty symbols of the sun brought to Thebes, and one of them, nearly a hundred feet tall, is still standing in the Amon temple at Karnak, its surface of highly polished granite beautifully inscribed with hieroglyphs. The stone for the obelisks was quarried from the vein of pink granite at Aswan, being cut in one piece with incredible patience and skill. The great piece of rock was cut horizontally, and the work of the men battering away at the dark, undermost face was grim, gritty, and danger-

TEXT CONTINUED ON PAGE 62

The Nubians, whose land lay to the south of Egypt, were forced to supply the Pharaohs with slaves (like this manacled youth) and with auxiliary forces for Egypt's armies.

59

Against the steep cliffs of western Thebes, Queen Hatshepsut built her monumental temple, dedicated to

the supreme god, Amon. Behind the building, and driven into the rock, is the royal funerary chapel.

TEXT CONTINUED FROM PAGE 59

ous. The Deir el Bahri relief shows how the shafts, once they had been dragged from the quarries, were shipped down river on boats that were hardly longer than the shafts themselves.

The reliefs on the first terrace tell quite different stories. One illustrates a royal myth, the notion that the Pharaoh was divinely conceived—particularly important religious propaganda for Hatshepsut. Hatshepsut's mother, Ahmes, is portrayed sitting politely on a settee with Amon, who tells her: "Hatshepsut shall be the name of this my daughter whom I have placed in thy body. She shall exercise excellent kingship in this whole land." The little Hatshepsut is shown being shaped by the ram-headed god Khnum on his potter's wheel.

Shown in the second group of reliefs is the expedition that Hatshepsut sent to the land of Punt to bring back precious African products for the enrichment of her capital. The details are so clearly depicted that the whole story can be reconstructed. In the sixth or seventh year of her reign, a party was assembled under the leadership of Nehery, a Nubian. They left the Nile near Coptos, to the north of Thebes, and with their trading goods packed on donkeys, made the long, hot trek across the desert to the Red Sea. Upon reaching the sea, they embarked in two ships, cheered on by sailors hanging in the rigging of the huge square sails. They sailed down the torrid Red Sea coast, probably going ashore each night, until at last they reached the fabled land of Punt. The people they saw lived among palm groves in round domed huts with high-set doors that were reached by ladders. There had been other earlier Egyptian expeditions to Punt, and the natives came down to greet this one with wonder and enthusiasm. According to the inscriptions on the reliefs, "They were received by the queen of Punt, and the Egyptian sailors did not trouble to conceal their laughter when they saw the queen . . ." She was horribly deformed, with huge thighs and a cripple's harsh, strained face (see overleaf).

Nehery had an emblem of Hatshepsut displayed, and the lesser chieftains threw themselves on the ground before it. "They speak, praying for peace from Her Majesty: hail to thee, king of Egypt, female sun who shines like the solar disc." Then the envoy pitched his tent and made a presentation of beer, wine, meat, and fruit in the name of his Pharaoh.

In the trading that followed, the Egyptians doubtless had the best of the bargain. They offered faience beads

Queen Hatshepsut drinks from the udder of Hathor, the goddess who often took the form of a cow and who protected the city of the dead.

and other trinkets; in exchange, their ships were loaded with ebony, ivory, gold, leopard skins, baboons, and myrrh trees (for which Punt was famous), with their roots carefully protected for replanting. Many oxen must have been needed to help the men pull these treasures by sledge on the overland crossing back to the Nile. When Nehery and his men reached Thebes with their valuable cargo, they were received in state by Hatshepsut and Senmut. Standing behind the queen and her favourite was the young Tuthmosis III, burning incense before a giant statue of Amon.

Much has been made of Hatshepsut's suppression of her young nephew and of his resulting hatred for her. Later, he was to prove himself the best soldier and one of the most authoritative rulers in all Egyptian history, so his submission during the twenty-one years his aunt was in power is certainly puzzling. The belief that he felt a strong resentment is based on the fact that some successor to Hatshepsut obliterated the names and likenesses of the queen at Deir el Bahri and other monuments, and it seems likely that Tuthmosis was responsible. Perhaps he was. On the other hand, there is nothing to support the sug-

An obelisk erected by Hatshepsut is in the background of the photograph of Karnak at left; it is the tallest one still standing in Egypt. The other obelisk was set up by Tuthmosis I. As represented in the sphinx above, Hatshepsut— though a woman—is wearing the ritual false beard of the Pharaohs.

gestions that he was kept under restraint or that he finally deposed or even murdered Hatshepsut; and there is no doubt that he married her daughter.

Whatever the relationship between Hatshepsut and her nephew, it ended in 1482 B.C., when the Queen-Pharaoh died and Tuthmosis III began the independent reign that was to last over thirty years. From his mummy and from many portrait statues it is known that he was a small man, about five feet four inches tall, with a keen, alert face and the large nose characteristic of his family. When he took over the control of government, he found prosperity and a full treasury at home, but a crumbling empire in the Asian territories.

During the peaceful years of Hatshepsut's reign, chiefs and princes of Palestine and Syria had banded together against Egypt under the leadership of the king of Kadesh, whose strong fortress city was in western Syria, on the River Orontes. Behind this coalition, and a far more dangerous threat, was the increasing power of the Mitanni. Tuthmosis had decided that he would restore the empire won by his grandfather, and in a series of campaigns over a twenty-year period, he succeeded in pushing the Egyptian frontier farther and farther north. At last he was able to take his chariots across the Euphrates, crush the Mitanni, and force the Hittites, Assyrians, and Babylonians to pay tribute to his kingdom.

Tuthmosis III began his first onslaught against the

The great expedition to Punt made during the reign of Hatshepsut was recorded on the walls of her temple at Deir el Bahri. Trading between the two lands was a friendly affair presided over by the ungainly queen of Punt (opposite). In the wall painting above, men of Punt carry an incense-bearing tree, which has been uprooted and placed in a basket for transport. Behind them is a man with ostrich feathers and a basket of ostrich eggs. In return for such exotic articles, Egyptians traded beads and baubles.

king of Kadesh and his confederation during the second year of his independent rule. His declared purpose was to "overthrow that vile enemy and to extend the borders of Egypt as commanded by his father, Amon". He took a scribe with him to keep a record of the campaign, and this report was afterwards rendered into an immense hieroglyphic inscription on the walls of rooms he built around the inner sanctum in the temple of Amon at Karnak.

The king crossed the frontier of Egypt over what is now the Suez Canal, and after a ten days' march across the Sinai desert, captured the Philistine city of Gaza. Learning that the army of Kadesh was waiting for him at Megiddo (in the district of the biblical Armageddon), on the edge of the plains beyond the hills of Mount Carmel, he pushed on to the north. Another ten days brought the Egyptians to the foot of the Carmel ridge. Here a council of war was held to decide which of the three routes to take to Megiddo. The generals cautiously preferred either of two roads that reached the plains by relatively low and open passes, arguing that the direct way over the hills led through such narrow defiles that "horse would have to go behind horse, and soldiers and people likewise". But the king, according to the records, at once chose the short route over the hills, and his officers meekly submitted: "We are in the train of Your Majesty wherever Your Majesty will go. The servant will follow his master."

The Egyptian army formed into a narrow column, winding up through the harsh, scrubby limestone valleys. The king himself, standing in his golden chariot, made a shining figure. Around his body was his scale armour— a tunic covered with tiny bronze plates that glinted like the scales of a fish—and on his head he wore the Blue Crown with the golden cobra. The long line of chariots, arrows rattling in the big quivers, bumped, and sometimes overturned, on the rough mountain roads. The thousands of foot soldiers carried short, round-topped shields made of the hairy hides of cattle or deer stretched over boards, and for offensive weapons they had wooden-shafted bronze axes, spears, and daggers. Some carried bows, but the main concentration of this important weapon was with the men in the chariots. A powerful rearguard

Seizing a whole army of Asiatics by its collective hair, the young and vigorous warrior-king Tuthmosis III assumes a traditional pose in this wall relief. Beneath his feet are listed the names of the conquered peoples.

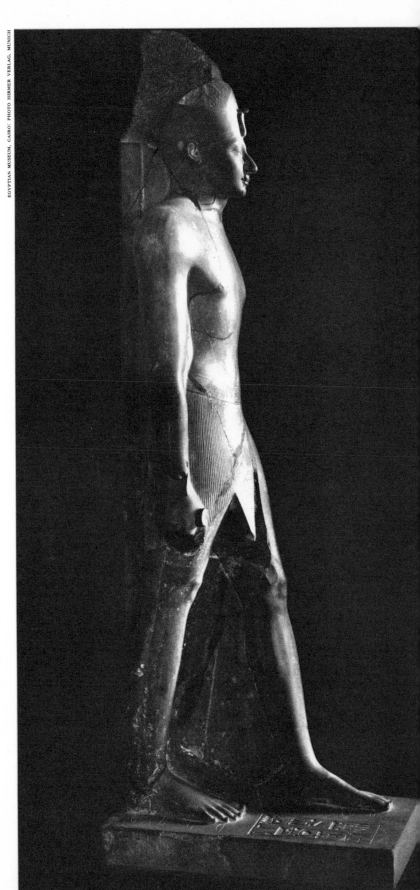

With his short neck and long legs, Tuthmosis III is portrayed realistically in this slightly larger than life-size statue. The four bows carved into the base of the statue by his right foot and the five by his left stand for the nine nations subject to Egypt during his reign.

followed in the wake of the heavily laden baggage donkeys.

The officers no doubt feared an ambush at every bend, but all went well. As the Pharaoh may have guessed, the king of Kadesh and his allies had expected the Egyptians to take one of the longer roads, and they were waiting for the invaders on the plain outside Megiddo. By the time the Egyptian rear was out of the hills it was near nightfall, and the whole army encamped. Tuthmosis exhorted his men to "prepare yourselves, make ready your weapons, for we will engage with that vile enemy in the morning".

In fact, the attack was delayed, perhaps because the Egyptians felt it would be better to wait for the auspicious new moon. When the appointed day dawned at last, Tuthmosis addressed his prayer to Amon and drew up his forces: one section was north of Megiddo, the other stretched south beyond the Kina brook, and the Pharaoh himself was in the centre. Tuthmosis fought with outstanding courage, and soon the kings of Kadesh and Megiddo and all the other allies leaped from their gold and silver chariots and fled back to Megiddo; finding the gates closed, they had to be hauled up the walls.

Unfortunately, the rich booty of battle was too tempting for the Egyptians. "Would that the army of His Majesty had not set their hearts upon looting . . . for they would have captured Megiddo at that moment, while the vile enemy of Kadesh and the vile enemy of the town were being hoisted up." However, the Pharaoh's army lost the opportunity and had to besiege the town for many months. Even when it finally fell, the king of Kadesh escaped, surviving to give more trouble on future campaigns.

The record of the Megiddo campaign is the earliest full account of a decisive battle. In spite of many later victories, Tuthmosis liked most to celebrate this one, evidently feeling that the rest of his career had depended upon it. From that time on he began a new policy that was to consolidate his conquests as he pushed on toward Mesopotamia. As each new city-state was conquered, he established a garrison, mostly made up of foreign mercenaries. In order to ensure future allegiance, he sometimes took the sons of petty kings back to Egypt. There they were trained to be his loyal lieutenants and later returned to their homeland. Tuthmosis also took great pains to defend and provision ports on the Syrian coast in order to secure safe passage for his navy, which transported troops and supplies.

As campaign followed campaign, the armies of Tuth-

Egypt gained much from Tuthmosis III's wars abroad—including the imported plants, trees, and animals recorded on this relief at Karnak.

mosis were shaped into a highly professional body, with separate and efficient organization for chariotry, infantry and navy, signals, accountancy, and the office of the quartermaster. Great soldier though he was, it is for his achievements as an organizer that Tuthmosis has made the greatest impression on later war historians.

On his fifth campaign, Tuthmosis struck successfully by sea at the rich maritime cities of northern Syria, and the next year he went on to capture his old enemy's strong and strategically important fortress of Kadesh. Now at last, in 1471 B.C., the way was open for him to settle his account with the Mitanni, his chief rivals for world power. Landing at the port of Byblos, he at once gave orders for the building of ships from the wood of the famous cedars of Lebanon. This was farsighted, for he knew he would need them to take his men over the Euphrates. But it was difficult to transport them, and in the end, he had them mounted on ox carts and sent on in advance of his troops.

Far from the sea, the ships were dragged in this fashion for some 250 miles.

All went according to the king's unusual plan. The broad, swift river was safely crossed, and Tuthmosis claimed that he was "the first of his army in seeking that vile enemy over the mountains of Mitanni, while [the enemy] fled before His Majesty to another far distant land". It was then, in the hour of his triumph over the greatest of his foes, that Tuthmosis III set up his stela near that of his grandfather, Tuthmosis I.

As had his grandfather before him, Tuthmosis paused in his journey to hunt elephants in the swamps of Niy, in northern Syria. After escaping unscathed during the war, the sport almost cost him his life. This, at least, is what is claimed by a general named Amenemhab who recorded in his tomb how he had come to his royal master's rescue. When a huge elephant charged the king, the brave general planted himself in front of his master and somehow cut off the elephant's "hand" (presumably its trunk) with his bronze blade.

Apart from hunting, which was done by all the Pharaohs, Tuthmosis may have been genuinely interested in wild life. Reliefs at Karnak show the plants and animals that he brought back from Asia, and he also had a rhinoceros shipped home from one of his Nubian campaigns.

Tuthmosis also found time for an ambitious building programme. In Karnak, in addition to the rooms inscribed with his famous annals, he raised a five-aisled pavilion, perhaps for the celebration of a *Sed* festival, and a colossal temple gate, or pylon, on which he is shown as a giant figure with mace upraised above a pitiful row of kneeling Asiatics. Like his aunt, he also erected a number of obelisks. Two of them still stand, but not in Heliopolis where they first stood: one is on the Thames Embankment in London, and the other is in Central Park in New York City.

No one can judge whether in the long run Tuthmosis' conquests were good for Egypt or whether they corrupted and overstrained her. But undoubtedly they brought great immediate wealth. Gold and goods of every kind poured in from countless tributary peoples, from Crete to Babylon, and south to the Fourth Cataract. With the age of conquest over, the Thebes of the later Eighteenth Dynasty became less martial, growing more extravagant, more highly cultivated and cosmopolitan. Splendour and luxury were to reach their climax during the long, peaceful reign of a later Pharaoh, Amenhotep III.

A delicate bronze mirror (above) was discovered in the excavation of a garrison fort on one of Egypt's routes of conquest into Ethiopia.

IV   SPLENDOUR

The pleasure-seeking sophistication of Amenhotep III's court is indicated in this funerary banquet scene by the easy gracefulness of the dancers and the liveliness of the musicians (who are shown frontally, an angle most unusual in Egyptian painting).

AND REVOLUTION

Tuthmosis III's great-grandson, Amenhotep III, became Pharaoh of Egypt in 1417 B.C., and while he inherited the aggressiveness and vigour of his warrior ancestor, his exploits took place on the hunting grounds rather than the battlefield. Once, on a wild-cattle chase, it was said that the king and his hunting party killed ninety-six wild bulls. And Amenhotep himself was said to have shot over a hundred lions single-handed. The actual score was doubtless improved to demonstrate the Pharaoh's superhuman strength—a common practice at the time. Similarly, Amenhotep's father, Tuthmosis IV, and his grandfather, Amenhotep II, had both been credited with impossible feats of strength: Amenhotep II was supposed to have rowed a large ship unassisted, with a thirty-four-foot oar, when the whole of his crew of two hundred men had, with ordinary human frailty, collapsed at their benches.

Amenhotep III may have killed most of the lions claimed for him, but, more important, he became a luxury-loving, self-indulgent king. If he ever led his army at all—which is doubtful—it was only on one campaign in Nubia.

Like some other members of his dynasty, he may have been dominated by an exceptional woman. Early in his life he broke royal protocol by taking as his queen and great wife a harem girl who was neither an heiress nor of royal blood, and who was probably the daughter of commoners. This was Queen Tiy, who remained Amenhotep's powerful consort throughout his reign, and who was still influential after the accession of their extraordinary son, the heretic genius Amenhotep IV.

There seems to be no doubt that Amenhotep III was fond of women. He had a large harem and many lesser wives, including several foreign princesses. One was from Babylon, another came from the royal house of the Mitanni, with whom Egypt was now on good terms. Even towards the end of his life, when he was fat and enfeebled, he married still another Mitannian princess, the niece of

Amenhotep III sent word of his new pleasure lake to officials throughout his land by means of scarabs such as the one above. The raised back (top) carries the king's name, and on the flat underside (bottom) is a description of the royal lake.

his earlier wife and the daughter of the reigning monarch. Her father, Tushratta, wanted her to be recognized as queen of Egypt, but apparently he had not reckoned with Queen Tiy, who retained her primary role. Indeed, in the following year, in honour of his great wife, Amenhotep built an enormous artificial lake twelve hundred feet wide and over a mile long and filled it with water flowing through a canal from the Nile. It seems unlikely that the queen, who in her portraits looks both quite feminine and remarkably determined, would have relinquished any part of the power she had enjoyed for so long.

During this time Egypt received a vast amount of tribute from her territories, but Amenhotep and his agents paid out a great deal of gold in gifts to his vassals and allies. He apparently preferred this expensive system of overlordship to waging campaigns. A letter from Tushratta is typical of the attitude of the Asian kings, who assumed that the Pharaoh was so rich he could pay out gold endlessly. "My brother," the Mitannian wrote to Amenhotep, "pray send gold in very great quantities, such as cannot be counted; my brother may send me more gold than my father got. In the land of my brother, is not gold as dust upon the ground?"

It was not. Nevertheless Egypt did have a good supply of gold in her eastern deserts, especially in Nubia, and Amenhotep III and Queen Tiy lived in luxury. They had sumptuous jewellery of gold and precious stones—bracelets, heavy necklaces, and girdles, all intricately designed and executed. Their furniture was embellished with patterns and scenes executed in gold, ivory, and precious wood-inlays. Caskets were crammed with rich gifts, and dressing tables were supplied with alabaster containers for cosmetics, oils, and scents, all carved with little animals and flower designs. When the royal pair drove out, it was in chariots plated with gold and drawn by splendidly caparisoned horses, their ostrich plumes tossing proudly at their heads. Painting and sculpture had reached new heights of elegance, and craftsmanship was at its most refined.

The king and queen began to build a new palace in western Thebes, south of El Qurn. Like other contemporary dwellings, their palace was constructed mainly of mud brick; stone was used only for the foundations and door frames, and occasionally for columns. But the new palace was spacious, and many of its rooms were charmingly decorated with paintings of birds and water plants. Ceilings were embellished with doves fluttering against a blue sky, and the whole interior was gay and naturalistic, somewhat in the manner of the famous palaces of the Aegean Sea peoples.

The pleasure lake that Amenhotep III had made for Queen Tiy was dug in only fifteen days (according to the stone scarabs on which all these details were recorded). The gardens around the lake were planted with flowers and aromatic shrubs and were surely the scene of many royal picnics and parties. At such celebrations the guests were waited upon and entertained by pretty girls who danced and poured wine, handed out flower wreaths or bunches of blue lotuses, and anointed the guests with sweet oils or presented them with small gifts from the Pharaoh. But the highlight of the entertainment was the music, played beside the water in the warm Egyptian night. Sometimes, little orchestras of girls with their harps, lutes, and double flutes, played on board a boat that floated gently along the water.

One such pleasure boat, a royal barge called *The Aten Gleams* ("the sun disc gleams") belonged to Queen Tiy. Among its rich and beautiful decorations were golden circles symbolizing the disk of the sun. These were observed

TEXT CONTINUED ON PAGE 78

The stone head of Amenhotep III below is perfectly preserved except for the insignia projecting from the Blue Crown, the warrior's helmet. The ebony head at left is probably Queen Tiy; the spike in her headdress was to secure her crown.

STAATLICHE MUSEEN, BERLIN

COURTESY OF THE BROOKLYN MUSEUM

75

Amenhotep III ordered these twin seventy-foot statues to be built in his likeness and set before his funerary

emple. Nothing remains of the temple now; the statues stand faceless in the fields of western Thebes.

by the queen's young son, who occasionally was taken for outings on *The Aten Gleams*. The prince was sensitive, studious, and passionately fond of nature. He watched the geese and the wild ducks on the lake; he liked to see the little black and white kingfishers hurl themselves into the water, and he enjoyed the pleasant feeling of the barge sliding among the water lilies. It seemed idyllic and utterly peaceful to the young prince. It may have been in these early years that the boy, struck by the painted symbols of the sun and by the order of the natural world, developed an idea that was to prove more powerful than the armies of his ancestors.

A mounting tension of ideas and personalities was already perceptible in Thebes: a tension between the two major sources of power. Ever since the beginning of the New Kingdom the Pharaohs had given treasure and great estates to the temple and priesthood of Amon-Re at Thebes. The nobles and the rich Thebans did so too, to enhance the glory of their city and to pay homage to the deity whom they had made the national god of Egypt. By endowing priests and mortuary chapels, they hoped to secure their own position in the after-life and perhaps also sought to win temporal power and royal favour as well.

As a result, the priesthood of Amon-Re grew, administering some of the largest temples in the world and controlling huge amounts of property with all the human beings and natural wealth that went with it.

The chief high priest of Amon-Re at Thebes became recognized as the primate of all Egypt, surpassing the former leadership of the priests of Re at Heliopolis and Ptah at Memphis. Tens of thousands of priests and their assistants now served Amon (only calling him Amon-Re to appease the Re factions in the north and the royal family). The Amon priesthood also had a large secular establishment, with its chief steward, its overseers of granaries, its cattle, craftsmen, peasants, police, and so forth. Thus it came to be that the religion of Amon, king of the gods, was a rival to the Pharaoh, king of the Two Lands.

The king and queen were aware of the threat to their power, and they did everything they could to restrict it. Apparently they looked to the north for support, for the priests of Re and Ptah were bitterly jealous of the Amon usurpers, and those of Re were especially eager to restore their traditional association with the throne.

To increase opposition to the priests of Amon, the worship of the Pharaoh as a divinity was encouraged. Amen-

Before the reign of Amenhotep IV, (at left, above) worship centred on Amon-Re (above), mightiest of the gods. When the young Pharaoh ascended the throne, he gave priority to the divine sun disc—the Aten. In the limestone frieze at left, Amenhotep (who took the name Akhenaten) worships his new god, who reaches down to him with hands attached to beams of light.

hotep began to erect colossal statues of himself that were not meant to be mere representations but were to be directly worshipped as his "living image". Soon, a statue cult grew up, extending to the south as far as Soleb, near the Third Cataract.

In Thebes, the statue cult grew more sophisticated. Amenhotep III began to build a mortuary temple in western Thebes; it was a little closer to the Nile than the temples of other New Kingdom Pharaohs, so that it stood just on the edge of the cultivated land. The temple was never finished, but the king did live to see and dedicate its most extraordinary feature—two gigantic seated statues of himself, each with a relatively tiny figure of his mother against his left leg and Queen Tiy against his right.

The statues were cut from one piece of stone and were originally seventy feet high and weighed far more than the largest obelisks. The marvelous feat of erecting them was the achievement of one of the most remarkable men of the court, a commoner who held the position of a scribe and was known as Amenhotep, Son of Hapu. Amenhotep was the New Kingdom counterpart of King Zoser's famous architect, Imhotep, and like him, Amenhotep was revered as a sage (and eventually worshipped in a small temple not far from that of his master).

The two towering sculptures, known traditionally as the Colossi of Memnon, were greatly admired by people of the ancient world, but it was not only their massive size that made them famous. In 27 B.C. an earthquake split the northernmost statue in two, and the stone set up a vibration, causing the colossus to "sing". Important visitors, even Roman emperors, came to hear the wonderful sound. But one of the emperors, Septimius Severus, decided to repair the broken colossus, and when the body and head were restored with several layers of stone, the gigantic statue lost its voice. The Colossi of Memnon still stand, overlooking the fields where peasants hoe their crops and drive their ox ploughs much as they did 3,400 years ago.

Amenhotep III's mortuary temple may have been unfinished partly because of trouble in the Asiatic provinces and partly because by this time the old Pharaoh himself was sick. He had celebrated his *Sed* festivals in the thirtieth, thirty-fourth, and thirty-seventh years of his reign. But gradually his strength failed, and death came in the following year. His son, who was still a boy at the time of his accession in 1379 B.C., was crowned as Amenhotep IV.

Amenhotep IV apparently suffered from a number of

glandular disorders and appears to have been rather effeminate. Certainly, he grew to have a most unathletic figure, with small, sloping shoulders, wide hips, and thin shanks. He loathed hunting, shooting, spear-throwing, and all the manly sports at which a prince was supposed to excel. Instead he was an artist, a poet, and a man of genius. And because he was an Egyptian, his genius inevitably found religious expression.

As Amenhotep IV grew up in the palace in western Thebes he was no doubt aware of the contest for power that his parents were waging with the priesthood of Amon. He must also have sympathized with their patronage of the rival priesthood of Re, with its royal tradition of worship of the sun god. In time he began to be interested in one particular aspect of this: the worship of the Aten, or the divinity of the sun's disc.

Since the time of Tuthmosis III's reign there had been a small temple and a priesthood of the Aten in Thebes. At the same time the name Aten began to appear more and more often in sacred texts, although it is often difficult to be sure whether the name refers to a deity or simply to the physical presence of the sun.

In his first years as the Pharaoh, Amenhotep identified himself with the Aten (although he also linked his title with the familiar Re). More and more he cut himself off from the worship of Amon. He took his first decisive step when he built a new sanctuary of the Aten at Karnak and covered the walls with a new divine symbol, a stylized picture of the sun's disc with rays that stretched downward

*Leaving the revels of Thebes be-
hind, Akhenaten sailed down the
Nile to build a new capital and a
new temple to his god. Although
little remains of that structure today, except for the ruined foundations at right, mural representations have survived. In the relief on the opposite page, columns
are shown dividing two courtyards;
altars and tables stand piled high
with offerings and food for the Aten.*

to the earth, ending in small human hands. It expressed
the belief that he was later to put into poetic words: the
idea that the sun extended love and protection and vitaliz-
ing power to bless mankind and every living thing—and
beyond them all, the young Pharaoh.

Up to this point the queen mother was probably in
sympathy with the son who was so unlike her in his un-
worldliness and his religious inspiration. It seems doubtful, however, that she supported him in his final decision
to make a revolution out of his religious beliefs. What pro-
voked it is not known, although afterwards the king made
a sombre reference to the priests of Amon doing deeds
more abominable even than those they had done in the
past. Whatever it was, Amenhotep took decisive action.
He changed his name entirely, proclaiming himself as
Akhenaten ("he who is serviceable to the Aten"). In an even
more momentous decision he resolved to move the capital
from Thebes and to found a new city away from the old
imperial luxury, the clutter of old gods and their idols,
and above all, of course, away from the dominance of
Thebes by Amon.

It was at about this time too that he took as his great
wife and queen a very beautiful young girl called Nefertiti.
We do not know who she was—she may have been a half
sister by some lesser wife of Amenhotep III. She shared
enthusiastically in her husband's new faith, and he came

Decorative palm gardens and fish-ponds with lotus flowers and ducks were popular in Akhetaten. Such natural delights are depicted in this contemporary tomb painting.

to love her with an openness and intensity that other Pharaohs would have despised or at least found unseemly.

In the sixth year of his rule Akhenaten and Nefertiti sailed down the Nile to found their City of God. They were young, they had their first child with them—an infant princess called Merytaten—and they must have been ecstatic about their sacred mission. About halfway to Memphis they came to a place on the eastern side where the cliffs curved away from the river to enclose a crescent of desert land. Nothing was there but some peasants' houses along the fertile bank. As Akhenaten himself had it recorded: "I found this place that belonged to no god or goddess, to no prince or princess—no one can lay claim to it." He spent the night in the royal tent, then drove in a gold and silver chariot to a point where the touch of the sun's rays told him that he should fix the southern boundary of his capital—Akhetaten, "Horizon of the Aten".

There he made offerings to his god and a proclamation to all who were with him. Rather touchingly he said that no man had advised him to come here. "No, it was the Aten himself, my father, who urged me to build this horizon city." He then declared, "To my father the Aten I shall build shrines and temples in this city. A royal palace shall I raise here." He added that he would have a tomb cut in the eastern mountains, where, after the long life that his god would grant them, he and Nefertiti and Merytaten would be buried, "And if I should die in another city . . . then I shall be brought back to be buried here in Akhetaten." Most ardently of all he spoke of the creative love of the Aten. "Each and every one of us he keeps alive and permits me every day to content my eyes with the sight of him when he shines forth in his temple in Akhetaten, having cloaked his limbs in beautiful rays of love."

In two years Akhetaten was ready for its inhabitants—the royal family, the court, and the priesthood and their followers—all of those who professed to believe in the Aten

Probably some of the men and women who went with Akhenaten to his new capital did not share his faith at all but were determined to make what personal profit they could from the venture. The king had gold and titles to

Not only was Akhenaten given to public displays of affection, but he had them recorded in limestone. Here he is shown in a garden with his queen, Nefertiti, and three of their children, all of whom are depicted as slim-shanked and round-bellied like the king. Elongated skulls accentuated by headdresses, thick lips, and long jaws were artistic mannerisms of the period.

83

84

The striking beauty of Akhenaten's queen, Nefertiti, is preserved in this painted bust in Berlin. The happy marriage of Akhenaten and his lovely queen was viewed (while it lasted) as a sign of the Aten's favour. Another harmonious scene from the period (at right) shows a man with a throwing stick hunting birds in the marshes of the Nile. He is assisted by a retrieving cat.

bestow; they would take them. Many others were probably unable to share Akhenaten's vision of a single god, the source of all life and love, who was never to be represented in human or animal form or to be bought off with spells and charms. Nearly all of them were "new men", promoted by the king from humble origins. The fact that even those who were of noble birth seem to have tried to conceal the fact, or at least to play it down, suggests that there was a genuine element of social revolution in the new world Akhenaten was trying to create. It also seems to have given more freedom and a higher status to women.

Indeed, the brilliant young king's mind was full of new ideas, ideas that have been viewed ever since as original contributions to man's understanding of his world. Even his central belief in the sun as a source of life and energy was a religious expression of what many centuries later was found to be a scientific fact.

Akhenaten also had a more sympathetic interpretation of *maat* than his predecessors. For him it not only meant truth in the conventional sense but an openness and an avoidance of hypocrisy, a determination to show things as they are. This affected not only the everyday life of the royal family and of all those subjects who imitated them but the style and content of the work of his artists.

Akhenaten and Nefertiti set an example of natural family life. They kissed and embraced their children in public, and they took them driving through the streets and let them urge the horses on. Also, they freely allowed themselves to be portrayed by painters and sculptors. For the most part (except for a period during the Twelfth Dynasty) the Pharaohs and their families had been portrayed only in a dignified and impersonal way, with idealized faces and figures. Now they appeared in informal scenes, and instead of idealizing the king's physical oddities, the artists seem to have been told to exaggerate them—fat belly, thin legs, and elongated head.

The whole spirit of Egyptian art was transformed, and Akhenaten himself was behind the change. Traditionally, figures and scenes were shown in a fixed, timeless way, as though frozen in eternity. Now there was movement, an active relationship between figures and groups and an intense sense of life and of the particular moment. Artists were much honoured at Akhetaten, and their houses and studios were situated in the best streets. Some of the finest

On the limestone block at right is an inscription of Akhenaten's hymn to the sun disc. It reads, in part:
How manifold are thy works,
Mysterious to our eyes!
O sole god, like whom there is
    no other!
Thou didst create the world ac-
    cording to thy desire,
When thou wert alone:
All men, all beasts, both tame
    and wild,
All that is on earth and walks
    upon its feet,
All that is in the sky and flies
    upon its wings.

examples of all Egyptian art were created during this period, among them the two superb and justly famous portraits of the beautiful queen Nefertiti (pages 84 and 136).

The transporting of the king and his loyal subjects to the new city was a tremendous undertaking, with hundreds of boats sailing down the river, laden with families and all their most precious possessions. By this time another princess, Meketaten, had been born to Akhenaten and Nefertiti, and a third, Ankhesenaten, was soon to follow.

Water and soil had been brought to the desert, which was cultivated until it was green with gardens and parks. The new city was laid out informally, with the comfortable houses of the wealthy standing in their own large gardens along two roads that ran parallel with the Nile. In some gardens there was a shrine with a carved stela showing the Aten spreading its rays about the royal family.

The main palace of the Pharaoh was above the river, looking across a terrace garden to the busy quays where boats and barges brought goods and passengers to the sacred city. From a specially designed window, called the Balcony of Royal Appearances, Akhenaten and Nefertiti, aided by their children, would hand out gold collars

TEXT CONTINUED ON PAGE 90

Two of Akhenaten's princesses are portrayed in the reliefs above. At the right, the Aten's hand holds forth an ankh *to Nefertiti while she kisses her daughter. At the left, sketched in partially carved stone, is another child who is eating a small duck while groping for fruit with her other hand.*

STAATLICHE MUSEEN, BERLIN

THE NEW ART OF AMARNA

Reverence for the past is a theme in Egyptian history, but Akhenaten's revolutionary reign was a violent exception. He built a new capital named Akhetaten to honour the Aten and himself, and there he moved with his family, wealth, artists, scholars, and court. The site is now known as Tell el Amarna, and the Pharaoh's era of reform is called the Amarna period. Akhenaten extravagantly ignored the past—two thousand years of customs, art, and religion —to satisfy his own beliefs and royal ego. The Aten rarely shone on anyone but the Pharaoh and his family, and everyone else had to worship the god-kings: Akhenaten and his successors. The scene on the left from the back of a throne shows Akhenaten's child Ankhesenaten and her husband, King Tutankhamon, receiving the Aten's benevolent rays; the figures have all the revolutionary aspects of Amarna art—bulging bellies, thick thighs, crooked necks, and slender calves. The same physical peculiarities are even more marked in the above study in painted limestone: another daughter, Merytaten, offers a bouquet of flowers to her relaxed, windblown husband, King Semenkhkara. Amarna art died soon after Akhenaten's death; the old gods reigned again.

TEXT CONTINUED FROM PAGE 87

and other awards to those who had served them well.

The king and queen also had a summer palace to the south of the town with an enchanting water garden set with pavilions and an indoor aquarium. Then, to the north, there was a third palace where birds and animals were displayed—perhaps to demonstrate the creative marvels of the Aten. There was a hall of tribute, a record office, a scholarly college, and, at the heart of it all, the huge temple of the Aten, where the god was worshipped in full sunshine in an open court. Akhenaten himself composed a superb hymn to the sun god for use in the temple services. This hymn, the greatest poetry surviving from ancient Egypt, finds an echo in the hundred-and-fourth Psalm of the Bible. How the words came down to the Hebrew psalmist some four centuries later no one can say.

For several years life at Akhetaten was near perfection. There was plenty of wealth, for nothing had been spent on wars, and property owners were required to supply the funds to support the temples. New hope and energy were generated by a new way of life, led by the inspiration of the royal family and their faith in a loving god. Artists of all kinds enlivened society and beautified the town, and the city itself grew more lovely every year as trees and gardens matured. And in the hearts of many of the new settlers there was a feeling—cherished by many human beings—that they were a "chosen people"

But after this first joyous period, unique in the history of the ancient world, things began to go badly for the Pharaoh and his followers. First, the second child of Nefertiti and Akhenaten, the Princess Meketaten, died. The Aten had not, after all, granted her long life. All the while, too, the Amon priesthood and the old nobility of Thebes had been conspiring against Akhenaten, and it may have been the discovery of some plot of theirs that made the king more fanatical in defence of his one true god. Orders were given to hack out the names of the old gods, and especially the name of Amon, from all the temples in the land. Many splendid old temples fell into decay, and the humble people of Egypt became upset and fearful.

Then, serious trouble began to develop in the Asian empire. It seems likely that Akhenaten was against war and the subjugation of foreign peoples. He regarded all nations equally as children of the Aten, for in his sun hymn he wrote: "You created the strange countries as well as the land of Egypt. You set every man in his place . . . Men speak in many tongues, in body and complexion they are

Artistic expression found its way into many aspects of everyday life in the Eighteenth Dynasty. This wooden, swivel-topped ointment container is inlaid with ivory and glass paste in a pattern of lotuses.

various, for you have distinguished between people and people."

Akhenaten's religious idealism and pacifist tendencies caused him to neglect the empire, and when the kings with whom he was allied in Palestine and Syria appealed for military help, none was sent. There was upheaval among the great powers too, for the Hittites were becoming aggressive and were expanding at the expense of the Mitanni. The loyalty of the Egyptian army and the defence of the frontiers depended largely on two men: Horemheb, a vigorous and experienced general who commanded the armies of Lower Egypt from Memphis, and Ay, commander of the king's cavalry, probably a brother of Queen Tiy and

Akhetaten has all but returned to the desert. In the foreground, below, are dovecotes of a present-day village, and beyond lies the plain on which Akhenaten's city, "Horizon of the Aten", once stood.

In this black granite statue, the headless figure of Tutankhamon is standing once more under the protection of the restored god Amon.

hitherto a stout supporter of the régime at Akhetaten.

Finally, there was tragic failure at the heart of the revolution—in the royal family itself. The Princess Merytaten had been married to a youth named Semenkhkara, and Ankhesenaten had been betrothed to the boy Tutankhaten, who may have been Akhenaten's half brother. These steps were important to the succession, as Nefertiti had borne six daughters but not one son. Then, either on personal grounds or from disagreement on religious and political issues, Akhenaten and Nefertiti, the embodiment of the ideal of the Aten, quarrelled and parted. Akhenaten took his son-in-law Semenkhkara as his co-regent, while Nefertiti went with her younger daughter and Tutankhaten to live in the northern palace.

Collapse was now inevitable. Semenkhkara went back to Thebes to make terms with the old order and the priests of Amon. But there he disappears from the records. And Akhenaten and Nefertiti disappear also. Like the figures in some glorious dream, they fade out of history. It is not known how or where they died; their tomb in the cliffs near Akhetaten stands empty. A mummy found at Thebes in a condition suggesting a hasty and perhaps surreptitious burial may be Akhenaten's—but even this is uncertain.

When his father-in-law and his brother-in-law disappeared, Tutankhaten was still a young boy, but because he was married to the legitimate heiress, he was crowned the Pharaoh at Akhetaten. However, Ay, the elderly officer who had long been close to the throne, exercised the real power. Ay had been an Atenist, and Akhenaten and Nefertiti had shown him and his wife every favour and had heaped them with gold. Yet with all haste Ay returned to Thebes and to the old religion, carrying the young king and queen with him. The final capitulation of the Atenist régime came when Tutankhaten's name was changed to Tutankhamon, and his wife's (Akhenaten's own daughter) to Ankhesenamon.

In a proclamation inscribed on the walls at Karnak, Tutankhamon said that all the way from Elephantine to the delta, the temples and shrines of the gods and goddesses had "fallen into desolation and become ruins overgrown with weeds, their chapels as though they had never been . . . The land was topsy-turvy, and the gods turned their backs on this land." So he "took counsel with his heart" on how best to placate Amon. As well as performing the expected rites and sacrifices on a colossal scale, Tutankhamon hit upon the means that Akhenaten would

King Ay, with a priest's leopard robe and an adze, performs a last rite, the "opening of the mouth" ceremony, on Tutankhamon's mummy.

have most hated: he set up jewelled statues of the ancient gods.

But ill luck remained with these last members of Akhenaten's family. Tutankhamon died at eighteen and left no son to succeed him. He would have had little historical significance had it not been that by chance, alone among all the royal tombs of Egypt discovered so far, the inner recesses of his burial place escaped grave robbers and survived to astound the modern world by their splendour (see pages 142–143).

Now Ay, the wily and ambitious councillor, found it easy to ascend the throne that for a decade he had controlled from behind the scenes. But Ay was an old man, and he reigned only a few years. It is not altogether surprising to find that he was succeeded by Horemheb, Akhenaten's former commander in the north and a tough professional soldier. His was an efficient but authoritarian and semi-military régime. He restored temples and put in soldiers as their chief priests. He also tried to check abuses in tax collecting and in the administration of justice, imposing frightful penalties, such as the cutting off of noses, on all those who broke his regulations.

As a conventionally minded soldier, Horemheb had probably felt little sympathy toward Akhenaten. Many of the royal possessions in Tutankhamon's tomb show the

The boy on the loping horse is part of an army camp scene from the tomb of Horemheb; the Amarna realism is still apparent in this military setting.

continuing influence of the art of Akhenaten, and a famous gold chair even displays the symbol of the Aten. But now, all signs of the heresy were to be wiped out. Horemheb claimed to have been the immediate successor of Amenhotep III, erasing the heretic Pharaoh's name from the list of kings and blotting out the king's portraits and titles. Meanwhile, the city of Akhetaten, after its brief moment of glory, was abandoned to the desert.

Horemheb led few military campaigns, so intent was he on stabilizing the internal affairs of Egypt. He probably made a treaty with the Hittites and frightened the Nubians, but his great interest was reform in the government and courts, and restoration of the Amon cult. After twenty-eight years of conservative rule, he died in 1320 B.C., and the Eighteenth Dynasty peacefully ended.

Another frieze from Horemheb's tomb shows prisoners of war, Semites and other Asiatics, bound in procession to be taken to the soldier-Pharaoh.

V

CONQUERORS' DECLINE

Horemheb had no heir, and in choosing his successor, he was determined to leave Egypt safely in the hands of one of his own officer class. He had already shown great confidence in a seasoned general named Paramesses, who came from a provincial town in the north-eastern delta. Paramesses was the son of a humble army captain who had risen to become commander of Egypt's land forces. Like his father, Paramesses had served in many public offices, and finally Horemheb had made him his vizier. At the king's death, in 1320 B.C., the vizier was given the Double Crown itself. Dropping the first syllable at the beginning of his name, he ascended the throne as Ramesses I, the founder of the Nineteenth Dynasty. Now, although Thebes remained Egypt's great administrative city, this dynasty ruled from a new capital, Pi-Ramesses, in the eastern delta on the site of the present-day town of Qantir.

The recent artistic and religious revolution and the subsequent violent reaction against Akhenaten's new society affected Egyptian culture as well as her imperial prestige. Painting and sculpture tended to be cruder, and architecture was more solid and grandiose than before. The written language became more like that of the common man and was interspersed with foreign words. Once again, as had happened at the end of the Middle Kingdom, social and political upheavals made Egyptians think less of pleasure in this world and more of security in the next. In the tombs of the well-to-do, earnest views of the afterlife replaced the delightful scenes of harvesting and grape gathering, of parties, musicians, and dancing girls that had been characteristic of the Eighteenth Dynasty. A favourite

A colossal head of Ramesses II, greatest of the Nineteenth Dynasty Pharaohs, rests at the feet of his funerary temple in western Thebes (opposite). In the wall painting above, Ramesses I is escorted by Anubis and Horus (left).

subject now was the judgment of Osiris, which showed a dead man's heart being weighed on the scales against the feather of Maat (see page 100).

Ramesses I was an old man at the time of his accession, and he was able to accomplish little during his short reign beyond securing the throne for his admirable son, Sety I. In the years to come, Sety was to raise Egypt once again from the doldrums of disunity and make her—for the last time—the most powerful empire in the ancient world.

Sety I's appearance is well known not only from a number of sculptured portraits but from a well-preserved mummy. Even after thirty-three centuries, it is possible to see that he was a strong, handsome, and forceful man. With his military upbringing he saw himself first and foremost as a soldier—and a soldier with a duty to restore the empire and Egypt's prestige abroad. He began to do so at once, leading strong forces into Palestine and Syria, and at the same time holding back the Libyans, who were now beginning to press against Egypt's western frontier. Sety's campaigns are celebrated in reliefs on the walls of the vast Hypostyle Hall at Karnak. He is shown there in the conventional pose of the all-conquering charioteer, running down his enemies (see page 104). But he is also depicted in a more unusual scene in which he stands holding two Syrian prisoners under each arm.

Sety I's greatest monument is the temple he built at Abydos, north-west of Thebes. This was the place where the head of Osiris, ripped from his body by the ferocious Seth, was supposed to have been buried. Abydos was a famous centre for pilgrimages and for cemeteries where the dead could lie near the king of the afterworld. Sety may have wanted to appease the priesthood of Osiris (after Akhenaten's denunciation of it and of the other traditional

TEXT CONTINUED ON PAGE 102

The two low-kneeling figures in the relief above are both Sety I presenting offerings to the gods of Heliopolis. In a less humble pose, the Pharaoh is shown opposite offering an image of Maat, goddess of divine justice.

98

From the beginning of the Eighteenth Dynasty an important object in the tomb of a wealthy person was a brightly illustrated papyrus scroll. These "Books of the Dead" recorded the funerary ritual of the Egyptians and the trials faced by the deceased on his way to the after-life. The scroll above from the tomb of Hunifer depicts two scenes. The first (on the left of the scroll) illustrates the weighing of the dead man's heart against the feather

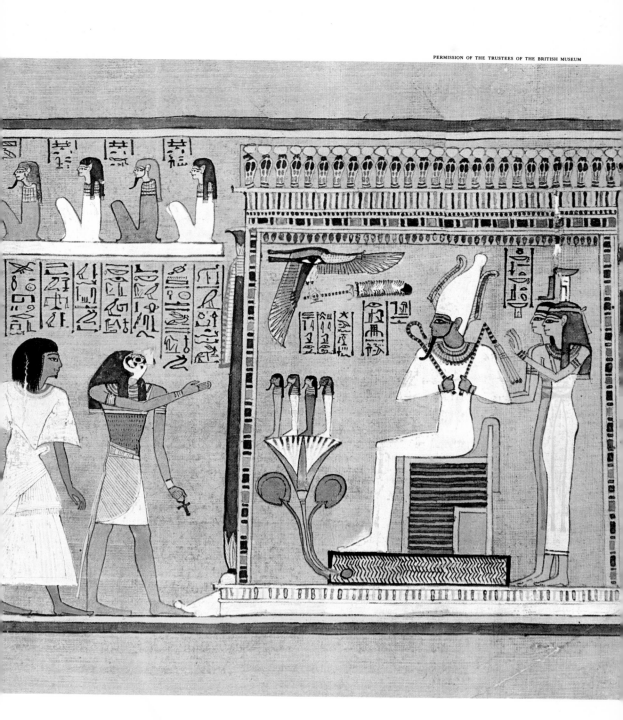

of Maat: that is, the worthiness of the soul to enter heaven is weighed against divine justice. Below the scale sits a monster to whom the heart would be thrown should the judgment be unfavourable. Hunifer (far left), holding the hand of Anubis, awaits the results of the weighing. In the next section, Hunifer, having received a favourable decision, is presented to Osiris by Horus. Osiris is attended by the goddesses Isis and Nephthys.

101

Ptah, one of the major gods in the Egyptian hierarchy, appears carved in relief at the temple of Abydos.

cults) as well as convince the people of the renewed might and true divinity of their Pharaoh. His temple was built as a national shrine, with chapels dedicated not only to Osiris, Isis, and their son Horus but to the foremost gods of Egypt—Amon, Re, and Ptah—and to the Pharaoh himself. The painted reliefs that decorate each chapel are exquisite, and they still retain their delicate colours. In each, the figure of the Pharaoh (either Sety or his father, Ramesses I) is shown presenting an offering of flowers and food to the gods. The reliefs are intricately carved, showing minute details of jewellery and headdresses, the folds of the women's gowns, and all the various insignia of the gods. In the chapel of Isis, the Pharaoh holds before the goddess a tray laden with cakes, meat, roasting ducks, and pomegranates. Isis herself wears a topless white shift, tied below her breasts with a red sash, and a vulture-winged headdress crested with cobras, horns, and the moon.

In a royal charter addressed to the priests and the other officials who were to maintain the temple, Sety listed a number of rights and privileges that these officials were to be allowed—such as freedom from arrest, the right to hunt, fish, and cultivate the land, and protection from seizure (presumably by local government officials)—which indicate a few of the hardships with which the Egyptian people then had to contend. More significantly, the charter also specified frightful punishments for any lawbreakers, including the same priests the charter purported to protect if they did not prosecute any and all offenders. Such harsh and dreadful threats foreshadow the moral decay of the years that were to follow Sety's reign.

Sety made a real effort, although it was as much in his own interest as for the benefit of others, to help the gold washers employed at mines near the Red Sea. These miners, working under extremely difficult conditions, had to travel many miles across a desert to get to the mines. Therefore, the king had a well dug and a small settlement built along the way in order to, in his words, "keep them alive, so that they may bless my name in years to come, and that future generations may boast of my energy and of one who is compassionate and regardful of travellers". In another inscription he enjoined any man from taking the gold intended for the temple at Abydos, declaring that

To the temple of Amon at Karnak, Sety I and Ramesses II added the great Hypostyle Hall; shown opposite is the length of the hall's central aisle.

In the two separate battle scenes above, Sety I is shown routing the enemy while ensconced in his chariot. The jumble of figures and chariots on the jagged remains of the temple façade at Luxor (opposite) depicts the successful campaign led by Ramesses II against the Hittite forces at Kadesh.

such thieves would be punished by Osiris, Isis, and Horus and by "all the great ones, the lords of the sacred land".

Sety reigned for a little less than fifteen years. When he died in 1304 B.C., he was succeeded by his son Ramesses, who had shared the throne with his father during Sety's last years. According to Ramesses II himself, his father had said, "Crown him as king that I may see his beauty while I am alive."

Ramesses II was evidently determined to emulate the strenuous efforts of his father to restore the empire, and he may even have seen himself as a second conqueror, like Tuthmosis III. His advance into Asia followed almost identically the paths taken two centuries before, for the available routes and the strategic points were unchanged. But while Tuthmosis liked to celebrate the Battle of Megiddo, Ramesses' favourite theme was the Battle of Kadesh.

Sety had captured Kadesh, but it had been retaken by the Hittites, who now controlled all of northern Mesopotamia and were battling with Syria. In the fifth year of his

An indefatigable builder, Ramesses II left his mark on Luxor. To the existing complex he added a large colonnaded court (above) that was decorated with six colossal statues of himself (four are visible).

reign Ramesses led a powerful army into western Asia. Its four divisions were named after the chief national gods— the Pharaoh himself was in command of the division of Amon. A month of marching brought his army to a hill from which they had a distant view of Kadesh, fortified with strong walls and gates and protected both by the River Orontes and two artificial moats. It appeared to be a formidable place, but there was no sign of the Hittites.

The next morning the Pharaoh set out with his Amon division and advanced to the Orontes. At this moment two men were brought to him who persuaded him that they were deserters from the army of the Hittite king, Muwatallis, and who said that the Hittite army was not at Kadesh at all but far to the north at Aleppo. Ramesses apparently believed them, for he pushed on so fast that his four divisions became widely separated. With his own force he set up a temporary camp north-west of the fortress. Most

At the outset of the Battle of Kadesh, Ramesses' troops were nearly routed by the Hittite charioteers. The relief at right from Carchemish, the Hittite capital, shows two agile warriors in their chariot.

of the chariot horses had been unharnessed and were being watered when the Pharaoh learned the alarming truth: the tale of the two men had been a trick; Muwatallis' army was just on the other side of Kadesh. Ramesses only had time to blame his officers for what had happened before the demoralized men of his Re division, who had been caught entirely by surprise, were swept past his camp in full flight. Then the Hittites attacked the royal camp. The vizier was sent to hasten on the division of Ptah, which never did arrive at the battleground. Meanwhile, according to Ramesses' account, abandoned by his whole army, he drove his single chariot against the 2,500 chariots of the Hittites. "They were three men to a pair of horses, whereas there was no captain with me, no charioteer, no shield bearer . . ." Then he reproached the king of the gods: "What ails thee, my father Amon? Is it a father's part to ignore his son? Have I not made for thee many monuments and filled thy temples with my booty?'' After this and much more, the king claims to have overcome the Hittites, trampling some under his chariot and driving many more into the River Orontes.

Although Ramesses' boasting seemed preposterous, it was once thought that a great Egyptian victory had occurred. But, a Hittite account of the battle has since been found in which they claim the victory at Kadesh, saying that the Egyptians were obliged to retreat to the south.

The truth probably lies somewhere between the two stories, for after further years of inconclusive campaigning, a peace treaty was drawn up between the two powers. In the treaty they agreed upon a line of demarcation, and each monarch promised to come to the support of the other if either should be attacked by an outside enemy. The alliance was reinforced by the marriage of the Pharaoh to one of the Hittite king's daughters, the Princess Manefrure. Ramesses interceded successfully with the gods to grant mild weather for the winter passage of the princess and her retinue through Syria and Palestine and then sent troops to escort her into Egypt. There was rejoicing and friendship between Hittites and Egyptians, and the Hittite princess was a great success.

Ramesses married Manefrure in 1257 B.C., an event that seemed to mark the end of his career as a warrior. From that time on, he led a luxurious, self-indulgent life,

Ramesses II had a variety of wives; one of his great wives and his favourite queen was Nefertari. She is shown opposite in a painting from her tomb offering a libation to Hathor. Political reasons induced Ramesses to marry a Hittite princess, who is at far right in the presentation scene above.

108

109

Lebanese chiefs (below) cut down their precious cedar trees as tribute for their conqueror, Sety I. Above, Ramesses' success against the Hittites is measured by counting the hands of his slain enemies.

enjoying the more peaceful pleasures of the kingship and celebrating nine *Sed* festivals. His reign was one of great prosperity for Egypt; it was also one in which scores of grandiose tombs and monuments were erected. Anyone travelling today in Egypt and the Sudan is often reminded of the power of Ramesses II. Of all the Pharaohs, he was the most relentless builder of temples; nearly half of those that survive can be attributed to him.

He was responsible for much of the construction at the new capital of Pi-Ramesses and for the building at Memphis of a large temple with colossal statues of himself. Perhaps his most famous work was the completion of the Hypostyle Hall in the temple of Amon at Karnak. In this astounding complex of buildings, in which so much of Egyptian history from Middle Kingdom times onward is represented, the hall of Sety I and Ramesses II is the most breathtaking of all. It consists of a central aisle of twelve columns no less than seventy-eight feet in height and so wide that a dozen men could easily hide behind one; the columns are flanked on each side by seven rows of smaller columns. In Ramesses' day the 5,800 square yards of this building were roofed, and light came in through clerestory windows above the central aisle. Today it is open, and to walk there is like wandering in a gigantic petrified forest, each trunk deeply carved with gods, hieroglyphs, symbols of Upper and Lower Egypt, and innumerable royal names in their oval cartouches. Men of all ages have marvelled at the Hypostyle Hall almost as much as at the pyramids. And although the building undoubtedly shows a greater pride in size than in grace or style, the gigantic scale of the place alone does indeed make it an awesome creation.

Ramesses also added a large court to the temple of Luxor, built by Amenhotep III, and across the Nile in western Thebes he built himself a mortuary temple now known as the Ramesseum. There he set up a fifty-seven-foot standing figure of himself carved from the granite of Elephantine.

In his Nubian territory, Ramesses erected great numbers of temples. Some of these are provincial work of the crudest kind, but outstanding among them are the temples at Abu Simbel, where the Great Temple of Ramesses and the Little Temple of Nefertari, one of his great wives, are cut out of the sandstone cliffs. The Great Temple penetrates the cliffs to a depth of 210 feet, and thousands of tons of rock had to be carried away before the sculptors could begin to carve the eight huge standing figures of the king, portrayed as Osiris. The walls are covered with reliefs of the Asian wars, and in the innermost sanctuary, four seated gods are hewn out of the rock: Re, Ptah, Amon, and Pharaoh himself. Outside, the stone has been carved into four sixty-odd-foot seated figures of the king gazing across the river towards the east. Although they might be called stolid, these sculptures have a calmness and dignity that are extremely impressive (see overleaf).

In contrast, Nefertari's Little Temple is full of feminine touches. It is dedicated to the goddess Hathor, and on the façade, figures of the king, the queen, and the goddess seem to be stepping out from narrow gateways in the cliff. The great beauty of these temples can best be appreciated when one approaches them by the river and sees them presiding over their quiet bay and the lapping waters.

The Hittite princess Manefrure found herself one among many other royal ladies, for during his long reign, Ramesses' marriages followed a most intricate pattern. He had already taken one other great wife before Nefertari, whose temple he raised at Abu Simbel, and he also married his mother and three of his daughters. He had at least a hundred, perhaps even a hundred and fifty, children, and out of all of his sons, the thirteenth, according to the list in the Ramesseum, was chosen to succeed him.

This was Merenptah, who came to the throne in 1237 B.C. He thought he was inheriting a prosperous and peaceful kingdom, but he soon found himself confronting a dangerous new enemy. The somewhat repetitious pattern of repressing native rebellions in Nubia and carrying out punitive campaigns in Asia was now broken; for the first time in her imperial history, the western frontier of Egypt was seriously threatened. The trouble was caused by great migrations of semi-barbaric peoples pushing down to the Mediterranean from the Balkan and Black Sea regions and penetrating into Egypt. Some of these people, or others whom they had dislodged, found homes along the North African coast of the Mediterranean.

The leader of this invasion was a Libyan, but he had in his army many of the Sea People, as the Egyptians called these new coastal settlers. Among them were peoples who are known from early Greek history—Sardinians, Sicilians, Lycians—and possibly even Etruscans and Achaean Greeks. They did not come merely as raiders but moved with their wives, children, cattle, and all their possessions, ready, if they could, to settle down. They sacked Egypt's western-frontier fortresses, but when they penetrated east-

TEXT CONTINUED ON PAGE 114

The enormous columns that form the Hypostyle Hall at Karnak record ritual scenes from the lives of Sety and Ramesses. The shafts of the columns also contain inscriptions left there by later kings.

THE SHRINES AT ABU SIMBEL

Ramesses II cut two temples out of a towering sandstone cliff at Abu Simbel. The façades alone are visible from the Nile (opposite). The larger of the temples (far left in the photograph) presents along its façade (above) four gigantic statues of the king. Carved at the feet of the statues are the immediate members of the royal family. The huge figures guard the entrance that leads to the Great Hall of Pillars (opposite, above). These pillars are in fact portraits of Ramesses as Osiris, and serve as supports for the ceiling. The ceiling is adorned with a painting of flying vultures. The smaller temple (far right in the photograph opposite) was dedicated to Hathor and the king's great wife Nefertari. This façade is decorated with colossal statues—four of Ramesses and two of Nefertari. The Nile, whose waters are rising because of Egypt's new Aswan Dam, will soon cover the lower levels. After the monuments have been removed to the top of the cliff from which they were originally carved, the king and his queen will continue to preside over the blue waters.

113

TEXT CONTINUED FROM PAGE 111

ward into the delta, Merenptah met and routed them. For the time being, Egypt was saved.

It was once thought that Merenptah was the Pharaoh mentioned in the biblical account of the Exodus. Now it is believed that the flight of the Jews took place when the Hyksos had fled the land centuries before.

Foreign attacks on Egypt slackened during the time of the undistinguished and short reigns that followed the sixty-seven-year régime of Ramesses II. But the irresistible pressure of great migrations was changing the whole ethnic pattern of the ancient world. Hittite power was shattered, and Egypt's former territories in Palestine and Syria were overrun by Philistines and Canaanites. Then, with the beginning of the Twentieth Dynasty in 1200 B.C., a furious onslaught against the Egyptian frontiers began. Ramesses III, the second king of the new dynasty, is usually granted the melancholy honour of being the last

The placid statues of Ramesses II overlook the construction of a dike that is to protect them from the rising waters during their removal. The new lake will be over three hundred miles long and will completely flood Abu Simbel's original site. The High Dam's crest will be two miles long and 360 feet high.

Ramesses III, shown in this tomb frieze with Isis, is considered by historians to have been the last great Pharaoh. Fighting defensive wars, he retarded the decay of his empire in the Twentieth Dynasty.

great Pharaoh of Egypt. He modelled himself upon Ramesses II, but there was no question of his fighting as far away as Kadesh. By now it was a grim struggle to protect the delta itself. The new Pharaoh had to deal simultaneously with renewed attacks by the Libyans and their allies in the west and a strong confederation of seafaring northerners who were trying to find new lands all the way from Syria to the western delta. Among them were the Philistines, who had settled along the coast of Palestine.

The confederation attacked Egypt by sea and by land. Again it was a true migration, the land forces being accompanied by ox carts crowded with women, children, and household goods. However, Ramesses III succeeded in repulsing them. On the walls of the massive mortuary temple he built at Thebes to compete with the Ramesseum, he shows a great sea battle, one of the first to be recorded in history. The enemy ships tried to sail up the Nile, but Ramesses' vessels stopped some, and his men boarded them. Others were showered with arrows from the river banks, and at least one was capsized (see below).

It was a glorious victory, and the subjects of Ramesses III may have felt that the power and the glory of the New Kingdom would be prolonged for ever. In fact it was already fading. The Egyptian armies that threw back the invaders were nearly all made up of mercenaries. Asiatics and Libyans filled important posts, and the Egyptians

themselves were becoming more and more conservative.

During the New Kingdom, Egypt had spent her energy on military conquests abroad and in keeping her own borders from being attacked. At the end of the New Kingdom, new nations with superior weapons were rising to challenge Egyptian supremacy not only in western Asia but within her own North African borders. Egypt's power was always dependent upon the strength of her Pharaohs, and the fortunes of the nation fluctuated with the influence of the particular king who dominated it. When a dynasty was weakened, so too was Egypt, and with the last of the great

Throughout the Twentieth Dynasty Egypt suffered from both foreign attacks and domestic turmoil. A line drawing shows Ramesses III's battle with the Sea People (below in the feathered headdresses). Upon the death of the last Ramesses, the kingdom split, and the powerful High Priest Herihor (opposite) seized the throne of Lower Egypt.

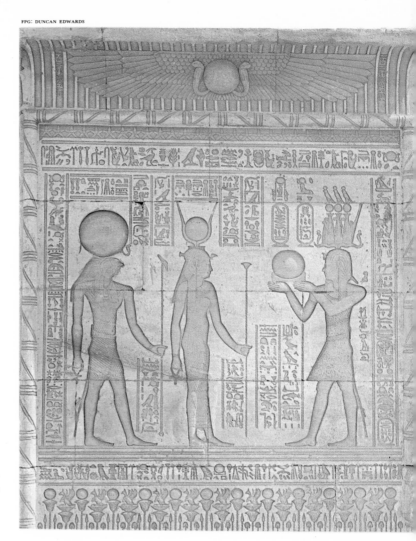

Egyptian sculpture maintained its traditional form even under the domination of foreign kings. In the relief at right the gods Horus and Hathor receive offerings from a Ptolemaic ruler. Although the outlines of the figures have been softened and the anatomy is better defined, the symbolic content and the use of the profile view remain unchanged from earlier days.

Pharaohs, the country commenced its final long decline.

The remaining kings of the Twentieth Dynasty, the last included in the age of the New Kingdom, were all called Ramesses. They sought greatness through the name, but through nothing else, and the reputation and authority of the divine Pharaoh diminished. The Egyptian people could no longer feel that they had a god in their midst. With the final Ramesses—the eleventh of the name—who died in 1085 B.C., the same kind of rivalry that had long ago alarmed Amenhotep III and Queen Tiy again endangered the throne of Egypt. This was caused by the great wealth and power of the high priests of Amon. Now, with the monarchy weakened, the priests could grow stronger than ever. During the last years of Ramesses XI, the High Priest

Herihor was even more powerful than his royal master, and at least within his precincts at Karnak, he had himself portrayed as an equal among the gods and with the Double Crown on his head.

Many more divisions and upheavals during the following centuries hastened the decline of Egypt. The two lands were broken apart once more, and there was a virtually independent kingdom in the far south under the governor of Nubia, the so-called King's Son of Kush. Curiously, this African territory had at last settled down so completely under Egyptian rule that a kind of old-fashioned respect for Egypt's traditional gods lingered on there. At the end of the eighth century B.C., a king of Kush went north and made himself the Pharaoh, bringing with him a revival of the old religion and a return to the virtues of *maat*.

The Kushites were able to bring some order once again to the country, and although twice invaded by the Assyrians from south-west Asia, Egypt recovered and was even able to enjoy another period of prosperity. This peaceful time was short-lived, however, for the Persians invaded the country, ruling it for nearly two centuries. They were followed by the Ptolemaic kings, descendants of Alexander the Great's general Ptolemy, who ruled Egypt after Alexander had conquered it. And finally, upon the death of the last Ptolemy, Egypt became a Roman province.

The Ptolemies took great pains to assume Egyptian ways and to emulate the lives of the Pharaohs. Traditional Egyptian culture persisted in the arts and crafts, and there was even an effort to revive the art styles of earlier periods. Architectural traditions were no less persistent. The temples on the island of Philae, for example, were partly built under the Roman emperors of the first and second centuries A.D., yet it is hard to tell that these are anything other than wholly Egyptian. There, still, are the gods and goddesses with their horns, their falcon heads, their discs of the sun, and there too is the ruler wearing the Red and the White crowns.

Although the Greek historian Herodotus went to Egypt when it was under Persian rule, he found the people still amazingly arrogant. No Egyptian might kiss a Greek or even use a Greek knife. Even Herodotus felt such awe for the Egyptian past that he almost accepted their opinion of themselves, and he began his account of their land: "Now I shall speak at some length about Egypt because it offers many wonderful things and contains works which are more remarkable than those of any other land . . ."

COURTESY OF THE ORIENTAL INSTITUTE, UNIVERSITY OF CHICAGO

One of antiquity's mightiest conquerors, Alexander the Great, as portrayed by an Egyptian artist.

119

VI

GOLD OF THE PHARAOHS

The history of ancient Egypt has become a familiar part of the story of mankind. Many points are still disputed by historians, and a number of periods remain obscure. But now since the hieroglyphs have been translated, the campaigns and treaties, the dynastic and religious upheavals, and the developments in art and literature are as well known as if this ancient civilization had never faded into obscurity. Great figures like Hatshepsut and Akhenaten have come alive again, and even the less famous ones, such as the general who saved Tuthmosis from the elephant, are beginning to emerge as real individuals. Yet, a short time ago none of this would have been possible. Only in the past century and a half have the thousands of years of Egyptian history been laboriously pieced together by archaeologists and scholars.

The magnificence of Egyptian civilization was never entirely forgotten. The Minoans of Crete, the Sumerians of Mesopotamia, the creators of the first civilization in India, had all vanished without a trace, and the world was astonished when archaeologists discovered their existence. In Egypt, however, visible evidence of its culture remained. The Pharaohs, wanting their temples and tombs to endure for ever, built massively and in the hardest stone. Because of this, and because of their exceedingly dry climate, their buildings have survived more or less intact, reminding all travellers through the Nile valley that Egypt once supported a powerful and extraordinary civilization.

The Egyptians themselves were the first people to study their own ancient history. By New Kingdom times the buildings of the Old and Middle Kingdoms were already so venerable that they had come to be regarded as national

The treasures of Egypt are heaped in the foreground of this engraving commemorating Napoleon's Egyptian campaign. French soldiers are in the rear.

monuments, and visitors from all parts of the land flocked to see Egypt's wondrous monuments.

In later times the pyramids and the temples continued to be admired, and Greek and Roman historians wrote down what little was remembered of the history of the Pharaohs. Some of these classical authors used an earlier source, a history of Egypt that had been compiled by Manetho, a priest at Heliopolis during the third century B.C. Most of Manetho's history has disappeared, but it is known that it was full of errors and misinterpretations.

Gradually the age of the Pharaohs slipped into the past. The last known hieroglyphic inscription was cut in A.D. 394, and when Egypt was converted to Christianity, some of the old pagan temples were made into churches. At the end of the seventh century, the Nile valley fell to Arab conquerors, and Egypt became an Islamic state. During the Renaissance in Europe, men became interested in the ideas and arts of the past. Wealthy and educated travellers made their way as far as Egypt and stared in wonder at the huge ruins on the banks of the Nile. However, they did not recognize

Not surprisingly, the ancient Egyptians were the first to study their own past. Sety I and Ramesses II are shown below on the Canon of Kings, a carved list of seventy-six of their ancestors. Sety and his son honour the dead with incense.

the kings and divinities carved on the walls, and they thought that the hieroglyphs were magical or religious symbols, not a script that could be read.

The first real advance in understanding the Egyptian ruins was made by Napoleon when he led the French armies into Egypt in 1798. He had brought with him 175 scholars and artists who were to explore and record the painted scenes and the hieroglyphs on the ancient monuments while his soldiers conquered the Nile valley. His expedition proved to be a military disaster, but his cultural contingent was a success. When the scholars got home to France they published the results of their studies in thirty-six illustrated volumes. The impact of their discoveries was immediate and widespread and they exerted a great influence on the taste of the time. Sphinxes, palm-tree columns, and many other ancient Egyptian styles became fashionable and were used in the furniture and interior decoration of the French Empire period.

During Napoleon's campaign, one of his officers who was in charge of trench digging near Rosetta, in the delta, came upon a large stela of black basalt. One side of the stela was polished—and was completely covered with writing. This writing was divided into three sections: one in true hieroglyphs, one in the simplified form of Egyptian known as demotic, and one in Greek. The Greek section could be read, and it proved to be a decree in honour of Ptolemy V, carved for him around 196 B.C. It was almost certain that the other sections of the writing would repeat the same words, and the importance of the stone as a key to deciphering hieroglyphs was quickly recognized. Napoleon had an engraving made from the inscriptions and sent copies to scholars throughout Europe. Then, in 1801, after the French were defeated by the English, the stone was ceded to England—and it now resides in the British Museum in London.

The Rosetta stone is the most famous of all Egyptian antiquities. Its promise was fulfilled, for it did provide the major key to the secret of the beautiful, mysterious hieroglyphic script. The first important break-through was made in 1819 by an Englishman, Thomas Young, who used certain principles he had learned from studying the stone to spell out the name of Cleopatra from another inscription. This was enough to convince many scholars that in spite of their pictorial forms, hieroglyphs did represent letters. Among those who agreed with Young's conclusions was a young French linguist named Jean François Champollion.

This romantic painting by Antoine Jean Gros shows Napoleon pointing to the Pyramids, while defeated Mameluke knights beg for mercy. Awed by antiquity, he reputedly said, "Soldiers, forty centuries look down upon you."

A French engineer found the Rosetta stone in an old wall. The basalt slab is over three feet high and is nearly three feet wide. The inscription is in Greek at the bottom, demotic in the middle, and hieroglyphs on top.

126

Champollion was already familiar with the Egyptian language as it was written in early Christian times, and this knowledge, together with an analytical turn of mind, brought him rapid success. By 1822 he was able to publish some translations of the signs, and during the next ten years he prepared an Egyptian grammar and a dictionary. After more than a thousand years, the words of the ancient Egyptians could be read again, and the history and literature of one of the great peoples of the world was revealed.

One of Napoleon's men made this drawing of scholars measuring the face of Chephren's Great Sphinx.

This was a priceless gain for modern knowledge and understanding of an age-old heritage. But much of the rest of the story of the nineteenth-century discovery of Egypt was not so admirable. The rivalry between England and France, already manifest in the seizure of the Rosetta stone, became widespread. It was a matter of prestige for the national museums of Europe to possess Egyptian antiquities, and they were not particular about how they acquired them. While some respectable national expeditions were sent to the Nile valley to survey the monuments and record their inscriptions, many others were not so honest. Champollion himself went with an Italian professor south to the First Cataract, and a great German expedition under the scholar Karl Lepsius penetrated to Khartoum, but at the same time the consuls of the European powers and their agents competed with one another in pillaging all that they could lay their hands on.

One of the most extraordinary of these ruthless collectors was an Italian named Giovanni Belzoni who worked as an agent for the British consul. Belzoni was 6 feet 7 inches tall and was married to an equally large Englishwoman with whom he had performed a strong-man act in a circus before chance brought them to Egypt. His methods of obtaining antiquities were more or less piratical, but so were those of his competitors. On one occasion he was trying to carry off an obelisk from the island of Philae when he was held up at gunpoint by the rival agents of the French consul, who claimed the obelisk as theirs. Belzoni's own account of how he set to work to despoil a tomb makes stunning reading for modern archaeologists. "When my weight bore on the [mummy] of an Egyptian," he wrote, "it crushed like a band box. I sank altogether among the broken mummies with a crash of bones, rags, and wooden cases . . . I could not avoid being covered with legs, arms, and heads rolling from above."

This was only one example of the harm done by ruthless or indiscriminate collectors during the first half of the nineteenth century. Yet Belzoni did make some important contributions. He skilfully brought a colossal head of Ramesses II from Thebes to London, where it is now in the British Museum; he was the first to start to uncover the famous temples of Abu Simbel; and he also discovered the tomb of Sety I in the Valley of the Kings.

In the second half of the century, archaeological standards began to improve. In 1850 a French scholar named Auguste Mariette went to Egypt and was able to induce the viceroy there to set up a service of antiquities, with himself as director. Excavation was controlled, tomb plundering was forbidden (although it continued in secret), and a national museum was established in Cairo.

Mariette's methods of excavation and of publishing the results, though an improvement, were still inadequate, and it was not until 1880 that scientific standards of research were introduced by an Englishman, Flinders Petrie. Petrie insisted that excavators make an exact record of everything they found, however insignificant it appeared to be. He also developed a way of using pottery to measure the relative age of sites that could not be dated by other means.

Toward the end of the century, some Americans began to take an interest in the exploration of the Nile valley, at first as patrons, but later as active archaeologists. George Reisner, for example, was one of the great excavators of the 1890's, and James Henry Breasted was one of the first serious students of the intellectual and religious life of the Egyptians. Through the influence of such men as these, the famed Oriental Institute was set up in Chicago and was also provided with spacious premises at Luxor. In the mid 1920's, H. E. Winlock, excavating in Hatshepsut's temple at Deir el Bahri, found the shattered statues of the great queen that are now in the Metropolitan Museum in New York City.

Undoubtedly the most valuable work of archaeologists and scholars is the slow, unspectacular accumulation of scraps of evidence that reconstruct the past. However, everyone delights in the rich and dramatic discoveries that have punctuated the course of archaeological exploration with splendid bursts of excitement. Without them archaeology might seem a dull occupation to all except the experts. Egypt, partly because of its past wealth, but still more because of a climate so dry that even the most perishable things may be preserved, has had an exceptionally large share of such discoveries. The majority of them date from New Kingdom times.

The most ambitious undertaking of the nineteenth-century strong man and Egyptologist Giovanni Belzoni (far left in Arab dress) was the removal of the colossal head of Ramesses II from western Thebes to London. That arduous operation is depicted in the engraving above. In spite of the dozing gentleman in the contemporary view at left, Belzoni's Egyptian exhibition was enthusiastically received in London.

129

One of the first of such finds goes back to the old days of commercial plundering. During the 1870's, Mariette and his colleagues began to suspect that important tombs had been found that were being kept secret by the natives. Papyri, scarabs, tomb figures, and canopic jars were reaching the antiquities market in large quantities. At last, in 1881, Gaston Maspero, the new director of the antiquities service, became convinced that a certain Abd-er-Rassul Ahmed, who lived in a village near the entrance to the Valley of the Kings, was one of the plunderers. Although this man swore his innocence, Maspero had him arrested and tried. His fellow villagers gave testimony that he was the most virtuous of men, incapable of taking the least of antiquities, let along the contents of royal tombs, and he had to be released.

However, a quarrel arose between Abd-er-Rassul and his brothers, and later in the same year one of them went to the local ruler and said that a tomb had indeed been found, and that it contained not one or two but dozens of mummies. Maspero himself was abroad at the time, but a member of his staff, Emile Brugsch, hurried to the site at western Thebes and was led to a deep shaft in the rock on the south side of Hatshepsut's temple at Deir el Bahri (pages 60–61). Brugsch went down the shaft and into a long tunnel leading into a small chamber. Crawling along, with only candles to light the way, he found a gallery in utter disorder, scattered with alabaster and bronze vessels, painted coffins, mummies, and the funeral tent of a queen. On his hands and knees, Brugsch peered at the inscriptions on coffins and mummies and found that he was reading the names of some of the most illustrious Pharaohs

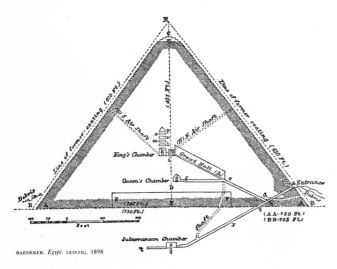

BAEDEKER. *Egypt.* LEIPZIG. 1898

Egyptologists often encountered considerable difficulty in penetrating the ancient tombs, due to complexities of design. The pyramid of Cheops is sketched at left: first was a sixty-two-foot descent from the entrance, then an uphill passage (blocked by granite to keep out thieves) through the Great Hall with its thirty-foot-high ceiling, then an antechamber, and finally the king's funerary chamber itself, 137 feet above ground level and walled in granite. The interior gloom is dramatized in the engraving at right of Napoleon's scholars exploring a passageway.

Description de L'Egypte, PARIS, 1809–26

of Egypt. Among them were Ahmose, Tuthmosis III, Sety I, and Ramesses II. As Maspero wrote soon after the discovery: "Monsieur Emile Brugsch, coming so suddenly into such an assemblage, thought that he must be in a dream, and like him, I still wonder if I am not dreaming when I see and touch what were the bodies of so many famous personages of whom we never expected to know more than the name."

Why had all these "famous personages" been crammed into this small tomb, while their own handsome burial places in the Valley of the Kings stood empty? The sealings of some of the mummies gave the answer. Some time after 1100 B.C., during the impoverished and disturbed reigns that followed the Twentieth Dynasty, tomb robbing reached an all-time high, and the royal graves were not spared. A Theban priest, horrified by the desecration of the bodies of the divine Pharaohs, gathered together as many as he could. Some he had wrapped in fresh linen and given labels of identity. Then he hid them away, together with as much of their grave furniture as he was able to rescue, in the tomb of a little-known queen. There they had remained until the nineteenth-century robbers resumed the pillage of their predecessors of three thousand years before.

The next spectacular find of New Kingdom treasures was made by an American. At the beginning of this century, Theodore Davis, a millionaire from Newport, Rhode Island, became fascinated by Egyptology. He was granted a concession for digging in the Valley of the Kings, and he had the services of a series of Englishmen who had been trained by the great Flinders Petrie.

In 1903 Davis and his archaeologists found the tomb of Tuthmosis IV, plundered but still containing some of the grave articles, including a chariot. Later, they located the completely looted tombs of Hatshepsut and Horemheb. In 1905 Davis found the entrance to a tomb in a space between the tombs of Ramesses III and Ramesses XI. The doorway was cut in solid rock and was blocked by mud and stones. There was a small hole in the top, however, and a little Egyptian boy, protesting that the spirits would get him, was lowered into the tomb on the end of a turban. There, at the entrance, he picked up a large stone scarab, a chariot yoke, and a carved staff. All had been covered with gold foil; it appeared that robbers must have brought them up from the tomb, believing them to be of solid gold, and then discarded them when they realized their mistake.

The next day the stones that blocked the entrance were

LEPSIUS, *Denkmaeler aus Aegypten und Aethiopien*, BERLIN, 1849–59

removed, and Davis, Gaston Maspero, and others, provided only with candles, went down a steeply inclined passage and a flight of steps before reaching a second doorway. This too had stones in front of it, but at the top of the door there was an opening to the next chamber. Holding their candles through the hole, the explorers could see a faint glimmer of gold. None of them were young men, but they managed to scramble over the stones and into an exceedingly hot chamber in which were two mummies. The faces of the mummies were exposed, undoubtedly by robbers who had torn off the bandages in a search for jewels. One was the mummy of an old man, the other was that of a calm, sensitive-looking old woman. Their gilded inner coffins had been pulled open, but they still lay in their funeral sledges, eight-foot wooden boxes coated with pitch. Around the top of the old man's sledge was a gold strip engraved with hieroglyphs. Davis held two candles so that Maspero could read the inscriptions. "Yuya!" he exclaimed. The American, recognizing the importance of the name, was so excited that he brought the candles close to the box. Maspero quickly pulled Davis' hands back. The pitch could have flared in an instant, suffocating them all in the tomb. Considerably shaken, the party scrambled out and waited until electric cables were brought in and the doorway unblocked.

They had every reason for jubilation, for they knew they had discovered the tomb of Yuya and Tuya, the aged parents of the famous Queen Tiy. Although the two old people were commoners, their relationship to the great wife of Amenhotep III had caused them to be buried in the royal valley. The interment was not only of great historical interest, but at that time it was the only nearly complete burial to have been found in the Valley of the Kings.

Large quantities of grave furniture were found in the tomb, and the robbers had even overlooked some pieces of gold. A handsome necklace of gold and lapis lazuli had slipped behind Yuya's neck, and there was a gold plate covering the incision the embalmers had made when they removed the old man's heart for separate preservation.

An unusual incident occurred while Davis' team was emptying the tomb. Everything had been taken out except

This engraving of Abu Simbel was made by Karl Lepsius to document his visit there in 1844. Like many historic sites in Egypt, the great temple of Ramesses II was drifted with sand blown in from the Western Desert.

Mummies of Yuya (top) and Tuya (below), the parents of Queen Tiy, were found in 1905. Although their tomb had been broken into previously by grave robbers, it still contained many lavish furnishings. The tomb was the most complete royal burial found until Tutankhamon's tomb was discovered.

a beautifully inlaid chair, a present to Yuya and Tuya from one of Tiy's children. The excavators heard the voice of an old lady insisting that she was quite able to make the descent into the chamber. It was the Empress Eugénie, widow of Napoleon III, then seventy-nine years old. The excavators apologized that there was no seat for her to rest upon. "This one will do very well," she replied as she sat down upon the priceless chair, which, fortunately, did not break.

Davis was now eager to find Queen Tiy herself, and two years later he believed he had succeeded. He and his team came upon another blocked entrance in the Valley of the Kings. The chamber was very small, but in addition to a badly smashed coffin, it contained a panel showing a queen worshipping the sun disc and fragments of a shrine with an inscription stating that it had been given by Akhenaten to his mother.

However, it proved not to be the queen's tomb, and it is still not certain whose it was. The coffin had been made for some queen or princess, but it had later been adapted to receive a man. This must certainly have been a Pharaoh, for the insignia of royalty, a bronze serpent (page 46) was found with the body. The royal name had been deliberately cut out from the gold bands around the mummy. Such a thing might well have happened if the body had been Akhenaten's. In the days after his death, when he was abominated as a heretic, his name was often erased. Furthermore, his name appeared on four bricks that had been placed in the tomb to protect the dead against evil spirits. Many experts are convinced that this poor grave was indeed that of the great religious reformer, who presumably met a tragic end. But anatomists have insisted that the skeleton is that of a much younger man than Akhenaten, and for this reason, other experts believe that the body is that of Semenkhkara, Akhenaten's son-in-law, who succeeded him briefly. However the argument may be settled, it is certain that this interment—poor, makeshift, and perhaps carried out in secret—reflects some part of the tragedy that engulfed Akhenaten and his family.

In 1907, the same year that Davis discovered this disputed tomb, a German expedition began excavating the city that represents Akhenaten's greatest achievement. The city of Akhetaten was built on the east bank of the Nile between Memphis and Thebes at a site now called Tell el Amarna. A certain flat-topped mound at this place was known to cover the remains of Akhenaten's city. Many

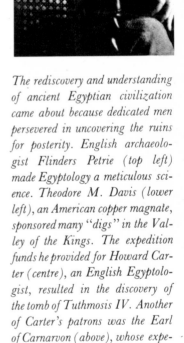

The rediscovery and understanding of ancient Egyptian civilization came about because dedicated men persevered in uncovering the ruins for posterity. English archaeologist Flinders Petrie (top left) made Egyptology a meticulous science. Theodore M. Davis (lower left), an American copper magnate, sponsored many "digs" in the Valley of the Kings. The expedition funds he provided for Howard Carter (centre), an English Egyptologist, resulted in the discovery of the tomb of Tuthmosis IV. Another of Carter's patrons was the Earl of Carnarvon (above), whose expedition found Tutankhamon's tomb.

of the inscribed boundary stones he had set up were still standing, and rock-cut tombs were in the surrounding cliffs, prepared for the royal family and the leading citizens of Akhetaten. These tombs contained scenes in relief showing the life of the city as well as many inscriptions, including the text of the wonderful hymn to the sun.

In 1887, a peasant woman digging among the ruins there had come upon hundreds of baked clay tablets covered with wedge-shaped impressions. When they were examined they proved to be the diplomatic correspondence of Akhenaten and his father, Amenhotep III. They were written in the cuneiform script of Mesopotamia, and nearly all of them were in Akkadian (a Semitic dialect of Babylonia and Assyria), the diplomatic language of that age. There were letters relating to the personal affairs of the royal house: the negotiations for the marriage of Amenhotep III with the Mitannian princess, and an invoice of all the gifts, from horses and gold chariots to embroidered sandals, that were sent with her when she finally went to Thebes. There were letters from Asian kings demanding more gold and other gifts from the Pharaoh. A large part of the correspondence told of the struggles and intrigues of the city states of south-west Asia. There was a whole series of appeals for military aid from Egypt's allies, sent in vain to Akhenaten. All the facts disclosed were of the greatest interest, for until that time no one had supposed that the rulers of the Bronze Age world maintained international diplomatic exchanges of this kind.

Flinders Petrie had investigated the spot where the tablets had been found and had uncovered some lovely palace paintings that may have decorated the royal harem. But large-scale excavation did not begin at Amarna until the Germans arrived in 1907. The fact that Akhetaten had

Excavations at Amarna in 1933 unearthed a magnificent unfinished head of Queen Nefertiti (at left) made of brown quartzite. The completed head would probably have been covered by a hood of a different material. Earlier excavations by the British had yielded a fragment of a wall painting (opposite) showing two princesses seated on several brightly patterned pillows.

been inhabited only for a very short time, and that it lay in desert land on which no later buildings were constructed, offered archaeologists a unique opportunity to explore a whole New Kingdom city and to study its architecture and layout. The work was cut short by the First World War but was later resumed by a British expedition. The greater part of Akhenaten's capital was eventually exposed, with all its palaces and temples, its houses both large and small, and its streets and wharfs. The excavators even came upon a model village of small uniform houses that were built for the workmen employed in making the tombs.

In a ruined temple of the king's summer palace, the original plan of the building was reconstructed in a most ingenious way. The walls of the building had been completely removed, but the cement floor survived. The English excavator, Charles Woolley, was wondering whether he could possibly detect where the walls had been when

he noticed some red lines on the floor. He investigated, and he found, to quote his own words, "When the cement foundation was dry, the builders had worked out on it the architect's plan: a cord dipped in red paint had been stretched taut along the line of each proposed wall, the middle of it lifted and allowed to come slap down on the cement, with the result that a red streak was left as straight as if it had been ruled; between two such lines the builder had laid his wall stones. We had no need to exercise our imaginations; we had before us the actual plan drawn out by the Egyptian architect."

Many charming things were found at Amarna, including walls and floors painted with plants and flowers, animals, birds, and butterflies in gaily coloured detail. One of these paintings shows two of the little princesses sitting in a garden (page 137).

The most important discoveries were found in the artists' studios. One, belonging to a sculptor called Tuthmosis, contained a whole collection of quickly modelled plaster hands, extraordinarily lifelike, which presented a vivid picture of the kind of people who lived at Akhetaten. There were also several sculptures of Akhenaten himself, some finished portraits, some preliminary studies, and some with his features so exaggerated that they were caricatures of the king.

But the greatest works of art were the two limestone heads of Nefertiti. One, unfinished, is lovely and full of feeling; the second, and more famous one, is painted and inlaid and seems to capture the strange, intense beauty of Akhenaten's once-beloved queen. Many people regard it as the masterpiece of Egyptian sculpture, and replicas of it have been sold throughout the world (page 84).

Beautiful as these works may be, for sheer dramatic excitement no archaeological find rivals the discovery of Tutankhamon's tomb. This was no chance discovery either but the reward of strenuous search.

When Theodore Davis had completed his last excavations, he wrote, "I fear the Valley of the Kings is now exhausted." But other archaeologists were still hopeful, believing that at least one more royal grave was still concealed

Artifacts like the one above, the seven-inch statuette of a young king (perhaps Tutankhamon), were the rewards of the painstaking work that went into the excavation at Amarna. In the Valley of the Kings, archaeologists found that Tutankhamon's tomb (right) had hardly been touched by vandals.

139

—that of Tutankhamon, the second son-in-law of Akhenaten, who had died in 1352 B.C. Davis had found a number of buried objects bearing the young king's name, but he believed that the tomb itself had been destroyed.

One of those who thought otherwise was Howard Carter, an English pupil of Flinders Petrie, who was working under the patronage of the Earl of Carnarvon. In autumn 1922, after digging with some success in the Valley of the Kings, he despaired of finding anything more and was already preparing to move elsewhere. Then, on November 4, when his men were clearing rubble near the entrance to the tomb of Ramesses VI, they struck the top step of a flight of steps leading downward. Full of excitement, they cleared the rest of the steps and came upon a blocked and sealed doorway. A cable was sent to the Earl of Carnarvon, and Howard Carter had to wait in painful suspense un-

The site of Tutankhamon's tomb was photographed (below) shortly after it was excavated. The passage to the tomb is hidden behind the low stone wall in the right foreground.

til his patron arrived on the site nearly two weeks later.

When the work was resumed, excitement ran high again, for seals at the base of the door bore the name of Tutankhamon. After so many seasons of disappointment, Carter was on the threshold of the very tomb he had most longed to find. Inside the door, the sloping passageway was filled with rubble, and there were signs that robbers had already been there. It was with as much doubt as hope that the excavators worked down toward the second sealed doorway at the foot of the passage. At last on November 26, they were ready to take down the blocking. It was, as Carter said, "The day of days, the most wonderful that I have ever lived through." With Carnarvon at his elbow, Carter held his light through the small hole they had made, and as his eyes grew accustomed to the dim light he found that he could see "strange animals, statues, and gold—

TEXT CONTINUED ON PAGE 145

The outer door of Tutankhamon's tomb was shut with a symbolic funerary seal (above). Filling a room called the treasury (left) was a wealth of objects including the god Anubis atop a gilt chest and the miniature coffin pictured top left.

141

ALL: EGYPTIAN MUSEUM, CAIRO; LEFT TO RIGHT: PHOTO HASSIA; PHOTO ROGER WOOD, COURTESY THAMES & HUDSON; PHOTO F. L. KENETT, COURTESY GEORGE RAINBIRD. LTD.; PHOTO ROGER WOOD, COURTESY THAMES & HUDSON

KING TUT'S TREASURE

On November 26, 1922, the English Egyptologist Howard Carter and his patron, the Earl of Carnarvon, opened a small door leading to the tomb of King Tutankhamon. It gave access to the greatest treasure that the ruins of Egypt had ever yielded. A long, narrow corridor led to the first and largest room of the tomb. Among the vast number of articles piled up along the walls of this room was a large funerary bed, one of whose gilded bed-posts was carved in the form of a lion's head (far left). The adjoining burial chamber contained the king's enshrined mummy. Tucked among the bandages of the mummified king, Carter found elaborate jewellery, including a gold cloisonné pectoral (above, left) inlaid with semi-precious stones. Connecting with the burial chamber, or "golden room", was the treasury. It overflowed with precious objects and was probably the richest of the four rooms in the tomb. The main treasure was a gilded canopic chest (above, right). The chest held four minature coffins that contained the Pharaoh's lungs, liver, intestines, and stomach, removed during mummification; the chest was surrounded by four goddesses (shown are Isis on the left and Serket right), guardians of the coffins. In the treasury, Carter also found a gilded wood statue of Tutankhamon as a harpooner (left), one of thirty-four statues symbolizing the king's activities in the after-life. Six years of work were required carefully to identify, catalogue, and then remove each of the objects from the tomb. Archaeologists can only guess at what incredible riches the tombs of great rulers must have held when a minor king like Tutankhamon was buried with such a dazzling array of treasure.

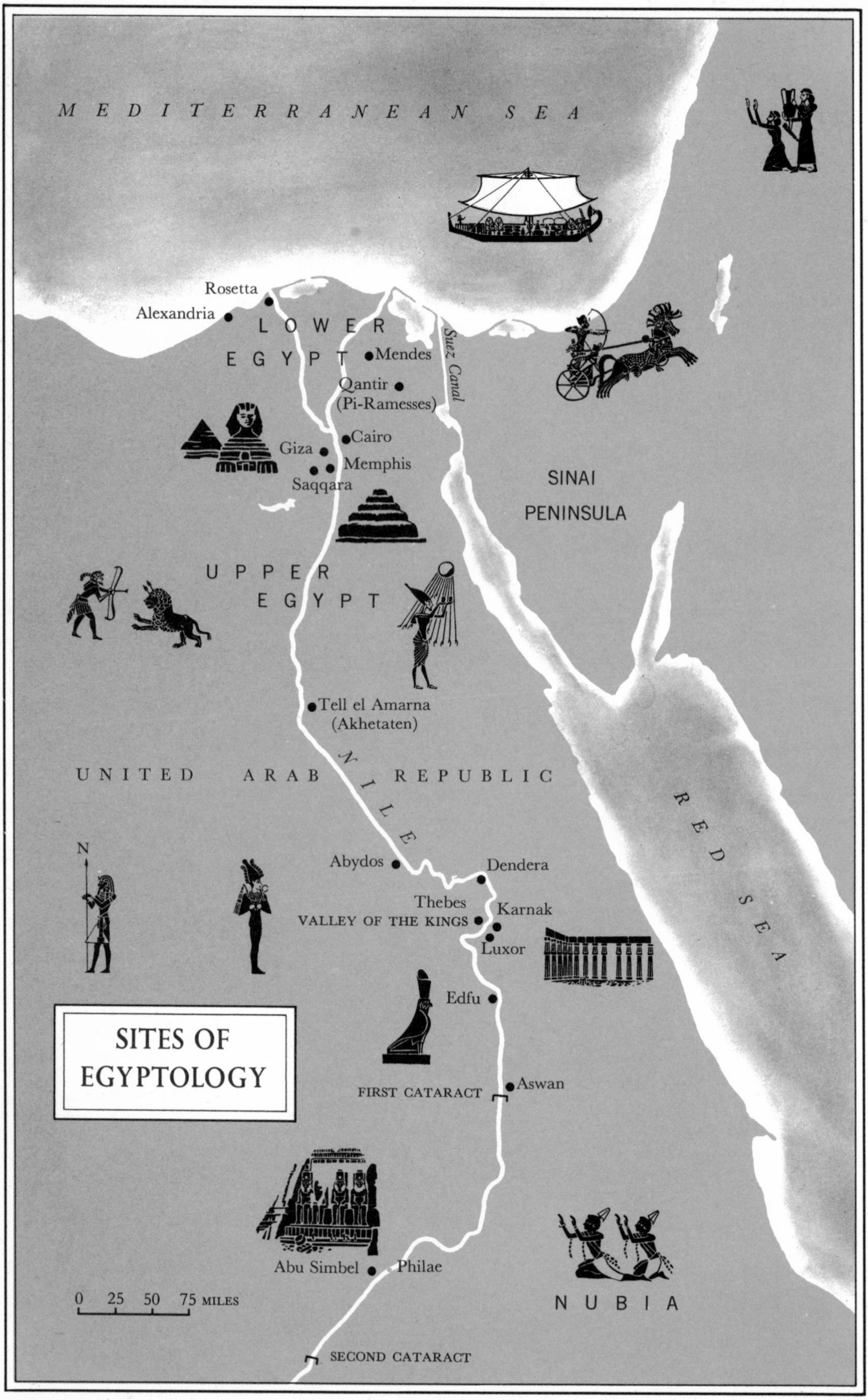

MEDITERRANEAN SEA

Rosetta
Alexandria
LOWER
EGYPT
Mendes
Qantir
(Pi-Ramesses)
Suez Canal

Giza
Cairo
Memphis
Saqqara

SINAI
PENINSULA

UPPER
EGYPT

Tell el Amarna
(Akhetaten)

UNITED   ARAB   REPUBLIC

NILE

RED SEA

N

Abydos
Dendera

Thebes
VALLEY OF THE KINGS
Karnak
Luxor

SITES OF
EGYPTOLOGY

Edfu

FIRST CATARACT
Aswan

Abu Simbel
Philae

0   25   50   75 MILES

NUBIA

SECOND CATARACT

TEXT CONTINUED FROM PAGE 141

everywhere the glint of gold". At last they had found a Pharaoh's tomb all but intact. It had been disturbed by grave robbers, but apparently they had been interrupted before they had had time to steal more than a few jewels. Although it was the tomb of an undistinguished king who had died at eighteen, it proved to be far more splendidly furnished, and was richer too in magnificent religious symbolism, than any archaeologist would have dreamed possible, even for one of the greatest Pharaohs.

The strange animals that Carter had seen were gold-plated lions, bulls, and hippopotamuses that formed the supports of three large couches, but these were only a part of the treasure piled in this anteroom. There were golden thrones marvellously ornamented, caskets full of jewels and other precious things, magnificent chariots, alabaster vases, and all manner of exquisite small personal possessions—even a farewell bunch of flowers.

Yet the anteroom with all its treasures was no more than an introduction to the wonder of the actual tomb. The statues that had immediately caught Carter's eye were two figures of the king standing guard on either side of another

The photograph at right, taken in the spring of 1965, shows work in progress at the "dig" sponsored by New York University in Mendes in the eastern delta. The excavators have found remains dating throughout Pharaonic times. Sites of historic interest that may be visited today are marked on the map opposite.

sealed door. After months of clearing out the anteroom, the excavators were at last able to take down the door. This time they were confronted by what seemed to be a solid wall of gold. It proved to be the outermost of four golden shrines that enclosed the burial place. The outer shrine was so large that it almost filled the burial chamber, which was itself embellished with painted scenes of the after-world. One within the other, the four shrines enclosed a massive stone sarcophagus, and inside that was a nest of three coffins. Each coffin depicted the king with his crown and insignia, and the innermost coffin was of solid gold. The mummy that lay at the heart of these eight containers was badly preserved, but wrapped in its bandages were scores of great jewels and amulets, while the head was covered by a superb mask, and the arms and fingers were heavy with bracelets and rings. In a third small room opening off the burial chamber, in a shrine protected by four golden goddesses, was the canopic chest. Even that was not the end, for inside this alabaster chest, the royal viscera had been placed in miniature coffins, again portraying the king and his insignia in gold and carnelian.

It is almost impossible to describe the marvels of Tut-ankhamon's tomb or even all the dramatic moments of its exploration—up to the opening of the last coffin in October, 1925. The galleries in the Cairo Museum, which now houses all the finds, are of course dazzling with gold. But it is not this alone that makes a visit to the museum an unforgettable experience. It is rather that the treasures reveal on one hand the daily life of a Pharaoh of the New Kingdom—there are his actual walking sticks and shoes, his couches, his tables and chairs, and scenes in which he is shown sitting with his wife, hunting, or driving his chariot. On the other hand, the many religious scenes, the vast array of gods and goddesses, and the potent religious symbols and texts make one realize something of the Pharaoh's divine life, of his existence as a god embodying the spirit of his people.

This—the coming together of humanity and divinity in one great national leader—was the meaning of Egyptian kingship. And for all its extravagance, Tutankhamon's tomb is a magnificent and undeniable statement of the spiritual brilliance and earthly glory that once was Egypt.

Near the pyramids of Giza (background) Cairo bustles along at a modern pace while the Nile, artery of Egypt's enduring civilization, flows steadily by.

This colossus of Osiris lies unfinished in the granite quarries at Aswan.

ACKNOWLEDGMENTS

The Editors would like to express their gratitude to the staff members of the many public and private collections in Europe, the Middle East, and the United States where material of special importance to this book was found. Particular thanks are owed to Mrs. Nan Sussman, Jean Keith, and Sarah Schwab of the Wilbour Library at the Brooklyn Museum, and to the following individuals and institutions for their generous cooperation:

The Department of Ancient Art, The Brooklyn Museum
The Metropolitan Museum of Art
The Museum of Fine Arts, Boston
The Art and Oriental divisions of the New York Public Library
The United Arab Republic Tourist and Information Centre, New York
The Oriental Institute, University of Chicago
Egyptian Museum, Cairo
Department of Egyptian Antiquities, British Museum
Griffith Institute, Ashmolean Museum, Oxford
Staatliche Museen, Berlin
Christiane Desroches-Noblecourt, Conseiller en chef des Musées Nationaux, Conseiller de l'Unesco auprès du Centre de Documentation et d'Etudes sur l'Egypte Ancienne, Cairo
Arpag Mekhitarian, Secretary General of the Fondation Egyptologique Reine Elisabeth, Brussels

Photographs by Roger Wood are from *Egypt in Colour*, published by Thames & Hudson Ltd., London, 1964
Maps by Argenziano Associates

FURTHER REFERENCE

Readers interested in further examining Egyptian art and artifacts will find exhibits in the Fitzwilliam Museum, Cambridge; the University of Durham Gulbenkian Museum of Oriental Art and Archaeology; the British Museum, London; the Manchester Museum; the Egyptian Museum, Cairo; and the Nicholson Museum of the University of Sydney.

For those who wish to read more about ancient Egypt and Egyptology, the following books are recommended:

Aldred, C. *The Egyptians*. Thames & Hudson, 1961.

Breasted, J. H. *A History of Egypt from Earliest Times to the Persian Conquest*. Hodder & Stoughton, 1905.

Carter, H. and Mace, A. C. *Tut-ankh-amen*. New York: Cooper Square, 1963.

Ceram, C. W. *Gods, Graves and Scholars*. Gollancz, 1952.

Desroches-Noblecourt, C. *Tutankhamen*. M. Joseph, 1963.

Drower, M. S. and Wood, R. *Egypt in Colour*. Thames & Hudson, 1964.

Fakhry, A. *The Pyramids*. Chicago UP, 1961.

Forster, E. M. *Alexandria: A History and a Guide*. Mayflower, 1961.

Frankfort, H. *The Birth of Civilization in the Near East*. E. Benn, 1959.

Gardiner, Sir A. H. *Egypt of the Pharaohs: An Introduction*. OUP, new ed. 1964.

Hayes, W. C. *The Scepter of Egypt*. OUP, Vol. I new ed. 1960, Vol. II 1959.

Herodotus. *The Histories*. Translated by A. de Selincourt. Penguin, 1954.

Kramer, S. N. *Mythologies of the Ancient World*. Chicago: Quadrangle, 1961.

Lange, K. and Hirmer, M. *Egypt*. Phaidon, 1961.

Mayes, S. *The Great Belzoni: Archaeologist Extraordinary*. Putnam, 1959.

Mekhitarian, A. *Egyptian Painting*. Translated by S. Gilbert. Zwemmer, 1954.

Moorehead, A. *The White Nile*. H. Hamilton, 1960. *The Blue Nile*. H. Hamilton, 1962.

Posener, G. *Dictionary of Egyptian Civilization*. Methuen, 1962.

Riefstahl, E. *Thebes in the Time of Amunhotep III*. Luzac, 1964.

Samih, Wali al-Din. *Daily Life in Ancient Egypt*. Translated from the German by M. Bullock. McGraw-Hill, 1964.

Smith, W. S. *The Art and Architecture of Ancient Egypt*. Penguin, 1958.

Steindorff, G. and Seele, K. C. *When Egypt Ruled the East*. CUP, 1957.

Wilson, J. A. *The Culture of Ancient Egypt*. CUP, 1956. *Signs and Wonders Upon Pharaoh*. Chicago UP, 1964.

Winlock, H. E. *The Rise and Fall of the Middle Kingdom in Thebes*. Macmillan, 1947.

EGYPTIAN MUSEUM, CAIRO

The ba *bird, part of a mummy's trappings, represented the dead man's soul.*

INDEX

Bold face indicates pages on which maps or illustrations appear

A

Abd-er-Rassul Ahmed, 130
Abu Simbel, 110, 111, **112–113,** 113, 114, **114,** 128, 133, **133–134**
  Great Temple of Ramesses II at, 110, 111, **112–113,** 113, 133, **133–134**
  Little Temple of Nefertari at, 110, 111, **112–113,** 113
Abydos, Egypt, 42, 98, 102
Achaeans, 111
Aegean Sea, 75
Africa, 11, 13, 14, 17, 32, 62, 111, 117, 119
Ah-hotep II, 33, 56
Ahmes, 56, 57, 62
Ahmes Nefertari, 56
Ahmose, 33, **33,** 35, 37, 53, 54, 56, 131
Akhenaten (Amenhotep IV), 17, 56, 73, 78, **78,** 79, **79,** 80, 81–83, 85–87, 89–95, 97, 98, 121, 134–138, 140
  Hymn of, 86, 90
Akhetaten, Egypt, 17, **81,** 82, **82,** 83, 86, 87, 89–91, **91,** 92, 95, 134–136, 138; *see also* Tell el Amarna.

Aleppo, Syria, 106
Alexander the Great, 17, 119, **119**
Alexandria, Egypt, 17
  Lighthouse at, 26
Amenemhab, 71
Amenhotep I, 54, 56
Amenhotep II, 56, 73
Amenhotep III, 17, 56, 71–75, **75,** 76, **76–77,** 79, 81, **83,** 95, 110, 118, 133, 135, 136
Amenhotep IV. *See* Akhenaten.
Amenhotep, Son of Hapu, 79
Amenmeses, 39
Americans, 131, 145
Amon, 21, 42, 46, 58, 59, 61–63, 66, 69, 81, 92, 95, 102, 106, 107, 111
  Temple of. *See* Karnak.
Amon-Re, 46, 47, 53, 78, 79
Amorites, 54
An, 29
Ankh, 29, 87, **87**
Ankhesenaten (Ankhesenamon), 56, 87, **88, 89,** 92
Anubis, 48, 59, 97, **97, 100–101,** 101, 141, **141**
Apuy, 45
Arabs, 123, 129
Archaeologists, 121, 127–131, 133–138, 140, 141, 143, 145

Armageddon. *See* Megiddo.
Asia, 13, 14, 17, 19, 22, 27–29, 32, 33, 53, 54, 66, 71, 90, 95, 105, 106, 111, 116, 119, 136
Assyrians, 54, 64, 119, 135
Astronomy, 23
Aswan, Egypt, 12, 19, 59, 148, **148**
  Dam, 113, 114
Asyut, Egypt, 32
Atbara River, 11
Aten, the, 17, 79, 80, 83, 85, 87, 89, 90–92, 95
  Hymn to, 86, 90
Atlantic Ocean, 13
Avaris, Egypt, 17, 32
Ay, 56, 91–93, **93,** 94

B

Babylon, 71, 73, 135
  Hanging Gardens of, 24
Babylonians, 64
Balcony of Royal Appearances, 87
Balkans, the, 111
Belzoni, Giovanni, 127, 128, **128–129,** 129
Berlin, Germany, 85

Bible, the, 37, 66, 90, 114
  104th Psalm of, 90
  See also Exodus, Joseph.
Black Sea, 111
Books of the Dead, 100, **100–101**
Breasted, James Henry, 128
British Museum, 124, 128, **129**
Bronze Age, 136
Brugsch, Emile, 130, 131
Byblos, Lebanon, 22, 70

C

Caesar Augustus, 17
Cairo, Egypt, 11, 12, 128, 146, **146–147**
  National museum in, 128, 146
Calendar, 40
Canaanites, 54, 114
Canon of Kings, 123, **123–124**
Canopic Jars, 51, **51**, 130, 143, **143**
Carchemish, Syria, 107
Carnarvon, Earl of, 135, **135**, 140, 143
Carter, Howard, 135, **135**, 140, 141, 143, 145
Central Park, New York, 71
Champollion, Jean François, 124, 127
Chariots, **endpapers**, 33, 47, 53, 55, **55**, 64, 66, 69, 70, 74, 104, **104–105**, 107, **107**, 108, 131, 136
Cheops, 11, 17, 26
  Pyramid of, **10**, 11, 26, 48, 130, **130, 131**
Chephren, 11, 17, 26, 127
  Pyramid of, **10**, 11, 25, **25**, 26
Chicago, Illinois, 128
Christianity, 44, 123, 127
Circuit of the Walls, 41
Cleopatra, 17, **118**, 124
Colossi of Memnon, **76–77**, 79
Coptos, Egypt, 62
Crete, 17, 22, 29, 71, 121
Crowns of Egypt:
  Blue (warrior king), 40, 41, **41**, 66, **67**, 75, **75**
  Double (Two Egypts), 40, **40**, 58, 97, 119
  Red (Lower Egypt), 22, **22**, 40, **40**, 46, 119
  White (Upper Egypt), 40, **40**, 46, 119
Cyprus, 22

D

Davis, Theodore M., 131, 133–135, **135**, 138, 140
Deir el Bahri, 59, 62, 63, 65, 128, 130
Diana, Temple of, 24, 26
Dynasties. *See* Pharaonic dynasties.

E

Egypt, ancient:
  Historical periods of: Pre-dynastic period, 17, 19; Old Kingdom, 11, 17, 23, 26–29, 33, 40, 44–46, 121; First Intermediate period, 17, 28, 32; Middle Kingdom, 11, 17, 28, 29, 31, **31**, 32, 42, 97, 110, 121; Second Intermediate period, 17, 32; New Kingdom, 7, 8, 11, 17, 19, 24, 33, 35, 37, 39–42, 44, 46, 47, 51, 53, 78, 79, 116–118, 121, 128, 131, 137, 146
  Lower, 17, 19, 22, 28, 33, 39, 40, 46, 91, 110, 117
  Upper, 17, 19, 22, 28, 32, 33, 39, 40, 46, 110
  See also Pharaohs.
Egyptian:
  Arms and armament, **endpapers**, 13, 32, **32**, 33, **33**, 53, **53**, 66, 71, 104, 107, **107**, 116, **116–117**
  Art and architecture, 7, 8, 12, 17–19, 22–24, 26–29, 31–33, 35, 36, 42, 47, 50, 51, 53, 55–63, 70–72, 74, 75, 79, 81, 86, 87, 90, 97, 102, 106, 108, 110, 111, 113, 115, 118, 119, 121, 122, 127–132, 136–138, 141, 143, 145; Amarna style, 17, 89, 94, 95, 136; obelisks, 58, 59, 63, **63**, 71, 79, 127; *see also* Crowns, Faience, Scarabs.
  Economics and trade, 8, 17, 19, 22, 23, 27–29, 31, 35, 54, 62, 63, 65, 70, 71, 74
  Farming, 8, 14, 17–19, 36, 79
  Language, 14, 97; *see also* Writing and literature.
  Religion, 8, **8–9**, 11, 12, 18, 19, 21, **21**, 23, 27, 28, 33, 35–37, **38**, 39–48, 50, 51, 53, **53**, 62, 63, 71, 78, **78**, 79, **79**, 80–83, 85, 87, 90, 91–95, 97, 98, 100, **100–101**, 101, 102, **102**, 105–108, **108–109**, 110, 111, 115, **115**, 118, **118**, 119, 121, 128, 131, 134, 143, 145, 146; *see also* Festivals, Funeral rites, Tombs.
  Science and technology, 19, 22, 23, 29, 32, 33, 42; *see also* Calendar, Mummification process.
  Society and government, 11, 12, **12**, 17–19, 22, 23, 27, 28, **28**, 29, 31, 32, 35–37, 39–44, **44, 45**, 47, 53, 54, 57–59, 63, 66, 68–72, 74, 75, 78, 80–83, 85, **85**, 86, 87, 90, 92–95, 97, 98, 102, 105, 107, 108, 110, 111, 114, 115, 117, 119, 121, 128, 131, 135, 136, 138, 146; *see also* Nomes, Viziers.
  Urban development, 18, 19, 35
  Warfare, **endpapers**, 8, 12, 13, 17, 19, **19**, 22, 27, 32, 33, 41–43, 47, 53–55, **55**, 56–59, 63, 64, 66, **67**, 69–71, 90, 91, **94**, 95, **95**, 98, 104,

104–105, 105–108, 110, **110**, 111, 114–116, **116–117**, 117, 121, 136; *see also* Arms and armament.
Egyptology, 7, 121, 124, 127–131, 133–138, 140, 141, 143, 145, 146
Elephantine, isle of, 59, 92, 110
Elizabeth I, 58
El Qurn, 36, 59, 74
Enene, 47
England, 124, 127
English, the, 128, 131, 135–137, 140, 143
Ephesus, 26
Ethiopia, 11, 12, 71
Etruscans, 111
Eugénie, Empress, 134
Euphrates River, 14, 17, 22, 56, 57, 64, 70
Europe, 13, 123, 124, 127
Exodus, the, 114

F

Faience, 23, 27, 31
Fayum Depression, 13, 14
Festivals, 37, 39, 40, 42, 44, 51
  Sed, 37, 41, 47, 71, 79, 110
France, 127
French, the, 121, 124, 126, 128
Funeral rites, 37, 39, 47, 48, **48–49**, 50, 51, 72, **72**, 100, **100–101**, 141

G

Gaza, Palestine, 66
Germans, 127, 134, 136
Greeks, 24, 111, 119, 122

H

Halicarnassus, Mausoleum of, 26
Hapù-seneb, 58
Harem, 39, 73, 136
Hathor, 59, 62, **62**, 108, **108–109**, 111, 113, 118, **118**
Hatshepsut, 17, 56–60, 62, **62**, 63–65, 71, 121, 131
  Temple of (Deir el Bahri), 58–60, **60–61**, 61, 62, 65, 128, 130
Heliopolis, Egypt, 17, 23, 27, 71, 78, 98, 122
Hemiunu, 26
Herihor, **116**, 117–119
Herodotus, 21, 119
Hetepheres, 26
Hieroglyphs. *See* Writing and literature.
Hittites, 54, 64, 91, 95, 104, **105**, 105–108, 110, **110**, 111, 114
Horemheb, 56, 91, 92, 94, 95, 97, 131

Horus, 5, 8, 21, 27, 36, **36,** 44, 45, 46, 48, 97, **97, 100–101,** 101, 102, 105, 118, **118**
Hunifer, 100, 101, **101**
Hyksos Pharaohs. *See* Pharaohs.

I

Ialu, Garden of, 50
Ice Age, 13
Imhotep, 17, 23, 24, 79
India, 121
Ipuky, 48
Isis, 36, **36,** 45, 47, 48, **100–101,** 101, 102, 105, 115, 143, **143**
Isit, 56, 58
Islam, 123
Italians, 127

J

Jews, 37, 90, 114
Joseph, story of, 32
Julius Caesar, 119, **119**

K

Ka, 51
Kadesh, 64, 106, 115
    Battles of (Tuthmosis III), 66, 69, 104, (Ramesses II), 70, 104, 105, **105,** 107, **107,** 108
    King of, 64, 66, 69
Kamose, 32, 33
Karnak, Egypt, 36, 37, 59, 63, **63,** 70, 71, 80, 92, 119
    Temple of Amon at, 59, 66, 102, **102,** 110; Hypostyle Hall of, 98, 102, **102,** 110, 111, **111**
    Temple of the Aten at, 80
Khartoum, Sudan, 11, 12, 127
Khnum, 62
Kina brook, 69
Kush, land of, 32
    King's Son of, 119

L

Lebanon, 110
    Cedars of, 70, 110, **110**
Lepsius, Karl, 127, 133
    Drawing by, **133–134**
Libya, 14, 111
Libyans, 28, 53, 98, 115, 116
London, England, 71, 124, 128, 129
Luxor, Egypt, 36, 37, 128
    Temples at, 104, **105,** 106, **106,** 110

Lycians, 111

M

Maat, 43, 44, 85, 98, **99, 100–101,** 101, 119
Macedonia, 17
Mamelukes, 125
Manefrure, 108, 111
Manetho, 122
Maps and charts:
    Chart of Egyptian chronology, **17**
    Chart of 18th Dynasty Pharaohs, **56**
    Map of Egypt, **16**
    Map of Egyptological sites, **144**
    Map of Pharaonic empire, **57**
Mariette, Auguste, 128, 130
Maspero, Gaston, 130, 131, 133
Mediterranean race, 14
Mediterranean Sea, 11, 19, 22, 111
Megiddo (Armageddon), Battle of, 66, 69, 105. *See also* Kadesh, Battles of (Tuthmosis III).
Meketaten, 87, 90
Memphis, Egypt, 17, 19, 22–24, 27, 29, 32, 41, 78, 82, 91, 110, 134
Mendes, Egypt, 145, **145**
Menes, 22
Mentuhotep II, 17, 28, 59
Merenptah, 111, 114
Merytaten, 56, 82, 83, 89, **89,** 92
Mesopotamia, 14, 35, 56, 69, 105, 121, 135
Metropolitan Museum, New York, 128
Middle Ages, 25
Minoans, 121
Mitanni, 54, 56, 64, 70, 71, 73, 74, 91
Mitanni Princess, 56, 73, 136
Mount Carmel, 66
Mummification process, 48, 51
Muwatallis, 106–108
Mycerinus, 11
    Pyramid of, **10,** 11
Myrrh trees, 63, 65, **65**

N

Narmer, 17, 22, **22,** 27, 40
    Palette, **22,** 45
Napoleon, 121, 124, **124–125,** 125, 127, 130
    Egyptian campaign of, **120,** 121, 124, **124–125,** 125
Napoleon III, 134
Nebamun, 48
Nefertari, 108, **108–109,** 110, 111, **112–113,** 113
Nefertiti, 8, 56, 82, 83, **83, 84,** 85–87, **87,** 90, 92, 136, **136,** 138
Neferura, 56

Nehery, 62, 63
Nekhbet, 46
Nephthys, **100–101,** 101
Newport, Rhode Island, 131
New York, New York, 71, 128
New York University, 145
Nile River, 11–15, **15, 16,** 17, 19, 21, 32, 35–37, 42, 43, 45, 51, 54, 57, 62, 63, 74, 79, 81, 82, 85, 110, 111, **112–113,** 113, **114,** 116, 123, 134, 146, **146–147**
    Blue, 11, 12
    Cataracts of the, 12, 19, 29, 32, 53, 54, 71, 79, 127
    Delta of the, 12, 14, 17, 19, 22, 32, 92, 97, 114, 115, 145
    Flooding of the, 12, 14, 15, 17, 18
    Valley of the, 12–14, 33, 35, 43, 121, 124, 127, 128
    White, 11, 12
Niy swamps, Syria, 71
Nomes, 19, 22, 42, 44
Nubia, 29, 32, 53, 54, 56, 58, 71, 73, 74, 110, 111, 119
Nubians, 8, 42, 43, **43,** 53, 54, 58, **58,** 59, 62, 95

O

Olympia, Greece, 24
Oriental Institute, 128
Orontes River, 64, 106, 108
Osiris, **38,** 39, 40, 42, 44–46, 48, 50, 51, 59, 98, **100–101,** 101, 102, 105, 110, **112–113,** 113, 148, **148**
    Myth of, 45, 46, 48, 98

P

Palestine, 14, 22, 27, 53, 54, 58, '64, 91, 98, 108, 114, 115
Papyrus, 21–23, 39, 40, 100, **100–101,** 130
Paramesses. *See* Ramesses I.
Pepy II, 17, 27, **27**
Per aa, 37
Persians, 119
Petrie, Flinders, 128, 131, 135, **135,** 136, 140
Pharaohs, 7, 8, 11, 12, 17, 19, 21, 24, 25–28, 32, 33, 35–37, 40, 42, 44–48, 50, 54, 56, 58, 62, 71, 86, 97, 114, 117–119, 121–123, 130, 131, 134, 144–146
    Hyksos, 17, 21, 32, 33, 35, 53, 58, 114
    Ptolemies, 17, 118, 119
    Succession of, 37, 39, 40, 43, 56
    See also names of specific pharaohs.
Pharaonic dynasties, 29, 32, 117
    1st, 17, 22, 23
    2nd, 21–23

3rd, 17, 23
4th, 17, 24, 26, 27
5th, 17, 26, 27
6th, 27
11th, 17, 28
12th, 29, 86
13th, 32
18th, 51, 54, 56, **56,** 71, 95, 97, 100
19th, 17, 39, 42, 45, 51, 90, 97
20th, 114, 115, 117, 118, 131
Philae, island of, 119
  Obelisk on, 127
  Temple on, 119
Philistines, 66, 114, 115
Phoenecians, 54
Pi-Ramesses, Egypt, 17, 97, 110
Priesthood, 37, 48, 117, 122, 131
  Of Amon, 58, 80, 81, 90, 92, 118
  Of Amon-Re, 78
  Of the Aten, 80, 83
  Of Isis, 102
  Of Osiris, 98
  Of Re, 80
Ptah, 78, 102, **102,** 107, 111
Ptolemies. *See* Pharaohs.
Ptolemy, General, 119
Ptolemy V, 124
Punt, land of, 27, 62–64, **64–65,** 65
  Queen of, 62, **64,** 65
Pyramids of Giza, **10,** 11, 17, **17,** 21,
  24, **25,** 26, 27, 47, 48, 110, 122,
  130, **130,** 146
  Battle of, **124–124,** 125
  See also Saqqara, Step Pyramid at.

Q

Qantir, Egypt, 97

R

Ramesses I, 17, 97, **97,** 98, 102
Ramesses II, 17, 43, 47, **47, 96,** 97,
  102, 104, 105, **105,** 106, **106,** 107,
  108, **108,** 110, **110,** 111, **112–113,**
  113, 114, **114,** 115, 123, **123,** 128,
  128–129, 129, 131, 133, **133–134**
  Temple of (at Karnak), 97, **97,**
  110, 111, 115
  See also Abu Simbel.
Ramesses III, 17, 114, 115, **115,** 116,
  116–117, 117, 131
  Temple of (at Thebes), 115
Ramesses VI, 140
Ramesses XI, 17, 118, 131
Ramesseum. *See* Ramesses II, Temple
  of.
Re, 21, 27, 43, 44, 46, 50, 51, 59, 78,
  102, 107, 111
Re-Horakhty, 21
Red Sea, 62, 102
Reisner, George, 128

Renaissance, the, 123
Rhodes, 22
  Colossus of, 26
Romans, 79, 122
Rome, 17, 119
Rosetta Stone, 124, 126, **126,** 127

S

Sa Gaz, 54
Sahara Desert, 12–15, **15,** 36, 43, 53,
  62, 133
Saqqara, Step Pyramid at, 17, 23,
  23, 24
Sardinians, 111
Scarabs, 74, **74,** 75, 130, 131
Scribes, 29, **29,** 31, **31,** 44, **44**
Sea People, 111, 117
Sed Festival. *See* Festivals.
Sekenenra, 32
Semenkhkara, 56, 89, **89,** 92, 134
Senmut, 58, 59, 63
Septimius Severus, 79
Serket, 143, **143**
Seth, 45, 48, 98
Sety I, 17, 98, **98, 99,** 102, 104, **104–
  105,** 105, 110, 111, 123, **123,** 128,
  131
Seven wonders of the world, 24, 26
Shaduf, 45
Ships, 13, **13, 15,** 19, **19, 30–31,** 31,
  41, 51, 70, 71, 116, **116–117,** 117
Sicilians, 111
Sinai, Desert, 17, 66
Slaves, 31, 32, 45, **45,** 59, **59**
Soleb, 79
Somali, 27
Sphinxes, 17, **17,** 25, **25,** 59, 63, **63,**
  124, 127, **127**
Stone Age, 11, 19
  Neolithic period of, 13, 14
  Paleolithic period of, 13
Sudan, 110
Suez Canal, 66
Sumerians, 121
Syria, 14, 22, 54, 56, 64, 69–71, 91,
  98, 105, 108, 114, 115
Syrians, 8, 22, 42, **42,** 43, 55, **55,** 58,
  58, 95, **95,** 98

T

Tell el Amarna, 42, 89, 134, 136–138
Thames River, 71
The Aten Gleams, 75, 78
Thebes, Egypt, 17, 21, 28, 32, 33,
  35–37, 40–42, 46, 47, 50, 53, 56,
  57, 59, 60, 62, 63, 71, 74, 77–81,
  90, 92, 97, 98, 110, 115, 128–131,
  134, 136
Tigris River, 14, 22
Tiy, 56, 73–75, **75,** 78, 79, 91, 118,

133, 134
Tombs, **endpapers,** 7, 8, **8,** 12, 17,
  26, 30, 35, 47, 48, 50, **50,** 51, 82,
  83, 92, 94, **94,** 95, 97, 100, 108,
  110, 121, 127, 130, **130,** 131, **131,**
  133, 135, 138, **139,** 140, **140,** 141,
  141, 142, 143, **143,** 145, 146
Tushratta, 74
Tutankhamon, **cover,** 8, 46, **46,** 51,
  56, **88,** 89, 92, **92,** 93, **93,** 135,
  138, **138,** 140, 141, **142,** 143
  Tomb of, **endpapers,** 8, 51, **93,**
  94, 135, 138, **139,** 140, **140,** 141,
  141, 142, 143, **143,** 145, 146
Tutankhaten. *See* Tutankhamon.
Tuthmosis I, 17, 47, 54, **55,** 56–58,
  63, 70
Tuthmosis II, 17, 56–58
Tuthmosis III, 17, 43, 44, 53, **53,**
  56–58, 63, 64, 66, **67,** 68, **68,** 69–
  72, 80, 105, 121, 131
Tuthmosis IV, 56, 73, 131, 135
Tuthmosis (sculptor), 138
Tuya, 56, 133, 134, **134**

V

Valley of the Kings, 47, 57, 59, 128,
  130, 131, 133–135, 138, 140
Valley of the Queens, 47
Viziers, 17, 37, 42–44, 58, 97, 107

W

Wazet, 46
Weni, 27
Winlock, H.E., 128
Woolley, Charles, 137
Writing and literature, 17, 22, 28, 33,
  97, 146
  Akkadian, 135
  Cuneiform, 135
  Demotic, 124, 126, **126**
  Greek, 124, 126, **126**
  Hieratic, 29
  Hieroglyphic, 7, 29, **29,** 50, 59, 62,
  66, 86, 111, 121, 123, **123–124,**
  124, 126, **126,** 133

Y

Young, Thomas, 124
Yuya, 56, 73, 133, **134**

Z

Zeus, statue of, 24
Zoser, 17, 23–25, 79